EIFFEL:
AN INTRODUCTION

PRENTICE HALL
OBJECT-ORIENTED
SERIES

EIFFEL:
AN INTRODUCTION

Robert Switzer

Prentice Hall

New York · London · Toronto · Sydney · Tokyo · Singapore

First published 1993 by
Prentice Hall International (UK) Ltd
Campus 400, Maylands Avenue
Hemel Hempstead
Hertfordshire, HP2 7EZ
A division of
Simon & Schuster International Group

Printed and bound in Great Britain
Dotesios Ltd, Trowbridge, Wiltshire

Library of Congress Cataloging-in-Publication Data

Switzer, Robert.
    Eiffel : an introduction / Robert Switzer.
        p.   cm. – (Prentice Hall object-oriented series)
    Includes bibliographical references and index.
    ISBN 0-13-105909-2
    1. Eiffel (Computer program language)   2. Object-oriented
programming (Computer science)   I. Title.   II. Series.
QA76.73.E95   1993
005.13′3–dc20   92-42245
                                                                  CIP

British Library Cataloguing in Publication Data

A catalogue record for this book is available from
the British Library

ISBN 0-13-105909-2 (pbk)

1   2   3   4   5   97   96   95   94   93

Contents

Editor's Foreword

'Where can I learn Eiffel?' The question is increasingly often heard from software professionals and students who wish to understand the benefits of a 'pure' approach to object-oriented development based on sound software engineering principles. Until now the only answer involved either short introductory articles or treatise-size books.

Robert Switzer's *Eiffel: An Introduction* thus fills a clear need. Crisp, simple and matter-of-fact, it introduces the essential elements of Eiffel through a well-designed progression relying on many carefully crafted examples. No pompous metaphors here, no comparisons of objects with employees about to retire, but concise presentations of all the key facilities and their methodological implications.

The discussion, which covers the most up-to-date version of the language, is meant for readers who are already familiar with the basics of programming and programming languages, and concentrates on the less conventional aspects of developing software with Eiffel.

The text evolved from the author's teaching, and the resulting pedagogical approach will be appreciated by students and software engineers alike. Another major influence is that of one specific Eiffel implementation and library, Eiffel/S. Although this does mean that some aspects may be less relevant for users of other implementations, it makes the book benefit from the kind of consistency and thoroughness that can only be ensured by an insider's perspective.

This timely presentation will be welcomed by many current users of Eiffel, and will undoubtedly bring new members to the Eiffel community.

Bertrand Meyer

Preface

Object-oriented programming technology is currently in the process of replacing the technology of structured programming that was popular in the late 1970s and 1980s as a method of analyzing, designing and implementing software. Object-oriented methods have proved to be more suitable for producing designs that are close to the application domain and that are easy to modify as the application domain or the designer's perception of it change.

The book *Object-Oriented Software Construction* [Ref. 1] by Bertrand Meyer has been quite influential in accelerating the acceptance of this new technology. It states very clearly the problems that need to be solved and the ways in which object-oriented techniques can help to solve them. It illustrates these ideas using the object-oriented programming language Eiffel that was developed by Meyer.

In principle one can apply the ideas and techniques described in [Ref. 1] using any of the commercially available object-oriented programming languages. Eiffel, however, is the language that most consistently strives to achieve the goals formulated there and has for that reason steadily gained in popularity in recent years. In *Eiffel: The Language* [Ref. 2] Meyer describes the latest version of Eiffel (Version 3), which has a number of significant improvements compared to the version described in [Ref. 1].

Eiffel: The Language is, among other things, the formal definition of Eiffel Version 3. But it is not unlikely that a book with ca. 600 pages will frighten off someone just beginning to use Eiffel. Thus it seems that there is still a need for a book that can be given to someone who is unfamiliar with Eiffel and convince him or her that the language is in fact very easy and intuitive to use. Such a book should also demonstrate that one can use Eiffel to produce complex software with remarkably little effort. It should do so by presenting some meaty examples that illustrate the advantages of the object-oriented paradigm.

This book is intended to fill that need. It does not attempt to be an exhaustive presentation of the language Eiffel; for that, one can turn to [Ref. 2]. It presents those aspects of the language that anyone will need who is beginning to produce software with Eiffel. The special features that only an advanced Eiffel user will ever need are not treated or are only briefly mentioned. In addition, it presents two substantial applications written in Eiffel describing their construction step by step and showing why they were designed the way they were.

It is assumed that this is not the reader's first encounter with a programming language. Anyone who has used a structured procedural language such as Pascal or C will find many language elements of Eiffel quite familiar. These parts of Eiffel are therefore given a rather cursory treatment, emphasizing only those aspects that are unique to Eiffel.

A reader who has worked his way right to the end of this book and has understood the example programs should then feel competent to tackle even quite large software projects using Eiffel.

The book naturally falls into two parts. In the first eight chapters all the important parts of the Eiffel language are presented and illustrated using mostly fragments of Eiffel code. Chapters 9 to 11 form the second part. Chapter 9 discusses the problems of writing reusable software generally and how Eiffel can help to solve them. Chapters 10 and 11 present the two major examples – with the goal of producing reusable software always kept in view.

It is perhaps pedagogically unfortunate that no complete programs are seen until the patient reader has plowed through to Chapter 10. But that lies in the nature of object-oriented languages: one does not really write programs, one writes classes. The classes are the building blocks out of which many different programs can then be built. Thus, in the early chapters we are almost exclusively concerned with constructing classes.

The reader who becomes impatient to see 'a real program' might try skipping from Chapter 6 to Chapters 9, 10 and 11 on a first reading. The contents of Chapters 7 and 8, while not unimportant, are not essential for understanding the examples in Chapters 10 and 11.

In a few cases, particularly in the example programs in Chapters 10 and 11, features are needed that are implementation specific. At the time of writing only one implementation of Eiffel 3 is available, Eiffel/S from SiG Computer in Germany. A version from Interactive Software Engineering was announced at the beginning of the year but has not yet appeared. Therefore, when we use features that are implementation specific we shall point out that these are specific to Eiffel/S. We cannot describe how analogous constructs in other implementations will look.

Now a word about the difficult matter of gender. Today any author risks being accused of sexism who uses the masculine gender exclusively on the theory that it stands for both sexes (a theory that was still accepted twenty years ago). Two of the commonly used alternatives seem unacceptable to me. Always using both genders ('she or he', 'her or him') makes many sentences unbearably long-winded. On the other hand flight to the plural ('if the programmer examines their code') is illiterate and pusillanimous. I have settled for what seems to be the least offensive solution: alternating genders. Sometimes our hypothetical reader or programmer is masculine, sometimes feminine. I just hope nobody tries counting the occurrences to make sure that I maintained parity!

Finally, I wish to express my thanks to the patient students of my courses on

Eiffel and object-oriented programming. Their questions have helped to clarify my thoughts about how to explain an object-oriented language to others who have never encountered such a language before.

Robert Switzer
Göttingen, October 1992

Chapter 1

Introduction

A major function of computer programs is to describe a **model** or **abstraction** of some aspect of our world. Sometimes it is a part of the physical world we are trying to model: molecules, the spread of epidemics, the operation of an elevator, the queues of customers waiting for a teller at a bank. Sometimes the model describes an aspect of our mental world: a system of partial differential equations, symbolic algebra, natural or formal languages, even some aspect of human intelligence. We build such models for several reasons. One is that we may understand better the thing being modelled; the process of modelling serves to separate the really important aspects of the subject being modelled from those that are incidental or at least less significant.

Another reason for modelling is that we may use a computer to try out our model and see whether it is a good approximation of the thing being modelled. If our models prove to be sufficiently good we can then use them to perform work for us. We can test a new wing design for an airplane much more cheaply in software than by building a prototype wing and testing it in a wind tunnel. We can investigate the effects of nuclear fusion much less expensively and with less risk using software than by actually carrying out the fusion.

Now if we accept this job of modelling reality in software as one of the most important roles of programming, then clearly we need programming languages that are well suited to building models. If one thinks about what the constituents of a model are, one readily sees that, among other things, we need to be able to describe *objects*, the *relationships* that prevail between them and the ways in which they *interact*. The first programming language that was explicitly designed to support these concepts was Simula, which gave rise to a new generation of programming languages in which the objects and their relationships play the central role. These languages are collectively known as **object-oriented** languages. Languages that belong to this category are (besides Simula) Smalltalk, C++ and CLOS. A comparatively new entry in the field is the language Eiffel developed by Bertrand Meyer. Eiffel has in common with Smalltalk the fact that it was designed from the very first to be object-oriented. Most of the other

1

languages in this category are extensions of non-object-oriented languages with object-oriented add-ons.

More traditional languages such as Pascal or C or Fortran emphasize the routine (procedure or function) as the central concept of the language. In such languages one mainly programs routines. In the top-down style of programming one first describes the 'main' routine – the one that solves the given problem. Then one refines the main routine to a series of subroutines, each of which deals with some partial aspect of the main problem. Then each of these subroutines is further refined and this process continues until one has reached a level of refinement where the routines are so simple that they can be implemented directly.

In such languages it is in fact possible to build 'objects'. They are usually represented by *data structures*. However, the data structures tend to play second fiddle to the routines. They feature as the arguments that are passed to the routines to be manipulated by the latter. Or worse, they represent 'global data' that are manipulated by several routines. Thus the data structures are designed to be optimally suited for the routines that are supposed to work on them.

In object-oriented languages the tables are turned; the data structures (the objects) move to the middle of the stage. Here routines are used to describe the actions or operations that the objects are capable of performing – the behavior of the objects. Analyzing and designing software now has a very different character: instead of finding the 'main routine' to solve the given problem the software designer is concerned with identifying the typical objects that will play roles in the model. Once the objects have been identified one can try to specify their behavior. This naturally leads to the routines that will be needed.

This altered perspective on the design process has had beneficial effects that were probably not anticipated at first. As Meyer points out in [Ref. 1], the objects in an object-oriented model tend to remain much more stable over time than do the routines in a top-down design. This means that the model is much easier to maintain and to extend as needs change and expand. As an example, consider software that is supposed to handle accounts at a branch bank. We could describe it by saying that it is supposed to

- register deposits and withdrawals,
- print records of transactions on demand,
- produce statistics on a monthly basis.

Then it is clear that, in time and if the program is successful, quite different demands will be made upon the software; that is, very different routines will be needed. It might then be required to compute interest automatically, to warn the bank personnel if accounts are overdrawn beyond a certain limit, etc.

On the other hand, if we design the software around the objects it models, we will probably choose such objects as: checking account, customer, automatic teller, etc. If these objects are carefully designed their descriptions are unlikely to change over periods of many years, maybe even decades. They can then be combined in different ways to deal with differing tasks.

This last observation points to another area in which the object-oriented approach to software design has proved beneficial. For more than twenty years software designers have dreamed of building reusable software 'components'. These would be pieces of software that could be combined almost arbitrarily with one another (without the components themselves having to be altered in any way) in order to construct new, more complex components or systems. One thinks of the way that elementary circuit and logic elements are combined to build complex circuits, or even entire computers, with comparatively little effort. Software components based on suitably designed objects (or, more precisely, classes of objects) hold the promise of finally fulfilling this dream.

One of the prerequisites for the successful use of electronic components is the availability of specifications for the use of these components: the data sheets published by the manufacturers state what voltages must be applied to which pins with which tolerances, and also state what currents are guaranteed to be available at outputs and how large the delay times are. Without this information the components would be much less useful than they are. Using them would become largely a matter of trial and error. Software components also need something like these data sheets.

So far, Eiffel is the only object-oriented language that provides something of this kind. The Eiffel assertions make it possible to formulate the prerequisites for the use of a given object and also what the object promises to do for its user. Experience has shown that judicious use of these assertions makes one of the standard tools of the programmer – the debugger – nearly superfluous. We treat the Eiffel assertions in Chapter 5.

So programming has now become the process of finding appropriate classes of objects and designing these classes carefully so that they are correct (assertions) and sufficiently general that they can be used in more than one way. A further new idea introduced by the object-oriented paradigma that has helped in making classes reusable is that of **inheritance**. If an existing class C proves to need some specialization before it can be used for a given application, then it is not necessary to alter the class C. One designs a new class of objects D that 'inherits' from C, that is, it automatically acquires all the properties and behavior of objects in C, and specifically adds only those things needed in the new context, or specifically specializes those aspects of C that need to behave differently in the new context. This is incremental software development. One builds upon what is already there instead of starting from scratch on each new project.

The following chapters will describe how these ideas have been implemented in Eiffel.

Chapter 2

Names, Entities and Objects

Not surprisingly, in an object-oriented language like Eiffel the data objects play an absolutely central role. Most of this book will be concerned with the objects (and the classes of which they are instances). However, in the first two chapters we shall not even attempt to say what an object is. Rather, we shall be concerned with the question of how one talks about and manipulates objects in a formal way, that is, in a way suitable for a computer program. For the moment we shall pretend we know what objects are.

Every object has a well defined **type**. (Every object also belongs to a class, which is essentially the same thing as its type; more about that in later chapters.) We shall have a great deal to say about the Eiffel type system in what follows.

With a few exceptions objects are anonymous. One can generate arbitrarily many of these objects and then manipulate them in appropriate ways. But one needs some way of keeping track of the objects one generates – some sort of 'handle' that one can attach to them so as to be able to refer to them. We shall call these handles **entities**.

Each entity has a **name**. Names are purely syntactical elements and are represented by strings of characters in the Eiffel source text. The names of entities must conform to the usual naming convention: a name begins with a letter and consists of letters, digits and the underline character:

```
window1, window2, next_child, ...
```

We must make the distinction between an entity and its name for at least two reasons:

- Entities are not the only elements of Eiffel programs that have names. Classes and routines also have names.
- The same name can be used for different things in different contexts. Thus for example two different classes could have an entity with the name foobar. They are two quite distinct entities. Or we could have a function named empty in one class and an entity named empty in another class.

Figure 2.1 An assignment

Just as every object in Eiffel has a well defined type, so every entity also has a type which must be declared in the Eiffel text:

    x : T

introduces an entity with name x and type T.

We introduced the entities in order to have 'handles' to attach to objects. We shall say that an entity is **bound** to an object. We are not, however, allowed to bind an entity to an arbitrary object: the types must match. For now, let us say that an entity of type T is only allowed to be bound to an object of type T. In reality the rule is more general: an entity of type T is only allowed to be bound to an object of type *conforming* to T. However, we are not as yet in a position to define what 'conformance' means.

There are only three ways to achieve this binding. The first is quite familiar to anyone who has programmed in an Algol-like language such as Pascal, C or Ada – the so-called **assignment instruction**

    x := y

Here x, y are entities of the same type (modulo the matter of conformance) and this instruction means: bind the entity x to the object to which y is currently bound. Fig. 2.1 above illustrates this operation.

Actually we ought to say: the entity whose name is x is bound to the object to which the entity with name y is bound; but that is very clumsy and so we shall almost always act as if the entity and its name were the same thing, since that will rarely cause confusion.

In fact we shall go even further in abbreviating the way of speaking about entities and objects. It is still rather cumbersome always to have to say 'the object to which entity x is bound'. We shall therefore simply say: 'the value of x' and mean the object to which x is bound (i.e. the object to which the entity with name x is bound). In any given context it should always be clear what is meant by 'the value of x'.

Now the question naturally arises: how did the y above get bound to the object? If we answer 'by assignment' we are faced with an infinite recursion.

Somewhere there must be a *first* binding of the object to an entity. And here we come to the second way in which binding can take place: through creation. (The third method of binding occurs automatically when we call a routine; we will see that in Section 3.7.)

The creation instruction in Eiffel looks as follows:

```
!!x
```

We assume that x is an entity declared to be of type T. Then this instruction means: create a new object (instance) of type T and bind the entity x to it. This is quite analogous to the **new** operator in Pascal; and in C one achieves something similar with the function `malloc`.

One of the main tasks of the following chapters will be to explain the Eiffel types (and classes). But some of the types will be familiar to anyone who has ever written a program. These are the so-called **basic types**:

```
BOOLEAN, CHARACTER, INTEGER, REAL, DOUBLE
```

The basic types are different from all other types in several ways:

- The objects of these types are predefined. They existed, so to speak, already at the beginning of time. (In fact, however, the set of instances of these types, except for BOOLEAN, is implementation-dependent. No real computer architecture is capable of representing the infinitely many whole numbers, for example. How many objects of type INTEGER actually exist varies, therefore, from one architecture to another.)
- All objects of these types have predefined names (which, unlike the names of entities, do not conform to the name convention above):

  ```
  true, false, -37, 3.14159, ...
  ```

  The objects of the non-basic types, on the other hand, are anonymous.

Remark The language definition provides the type DOUBLE in addition to REAL. This type is supposed to represent 'double precision' real numbers. In the opinion of this author that kind of distinction would better have been left out of a high-level language like Eiffel. We will not mention DOUBLE again.

Two further types are not strictly basic types but are so important that they are generally given special treatment by the Eiffel system:

```
ARRAY, STRING
```

(Actually **ARRAY** is not really a type but, rather, a generic class; we don't want to go into such matters just yet.)

Other types can be invented and defined by the programmer.

A curious reader may well ask 'To what is an entity bound from the moment it comes into being until the first creation or assignment involving this entity?' If we leave aside for the moment the slightly complicated question of what it means for an entity to 'come into being', we can give a simple answer to the reader's question. An entity of basic type is bound to a **default** object:

```
BOOLEAN      false
CHARACTER    '%U'     (null character)
INTEGER      0
REAL         0.0
```

Entities of all other types are at first bound to *nothing*; one says they are 'unbound'. In Eiffel we express this by writing

```
x = void
```

And we can make x unbound with the assignment

```
x := void
```

One may imagine that for every non-basic type there is a predefined entity void which is never bound to anything (in particular !!void is not allowed).

If the reader has a queasy feeling that there are knotty philosophical problems lurking behind the entity void, then she is to be commended for her acumen. We shall nevertheless proceed to ignore these problems.

Obviously we create objects with the intention of manipulating them in some suitable way – of operating upon them. We thus need some way to express the operations we wish to carry out. The language therefore provides names for **operators**: these are formed out of non-alphanumeric characters such as

```
+, *, &, |
```

and so on. Exceptional in this respect are the predefined operators not, or, or else, and, and then and implies for the type BOOLEAN.

Two operators play a very special role in the language:

```
=  ,  /=
```

Both can be applied to two entities of the same (or conforming) type and produce an object of type BOOLEAN as their result. The expression

```
x = y
```

yields the result true if and only if x and y are bound to the same object (or have the same value, to use our abbreviated way of speaking). This can also mean that they are both unbound if they are not of basic type. The operator /= yields true if and only if the entities are bound to different objects. This can also mean that one is bound and the other unbound.

The programmer who defines non-basic types will also create appropriate operators for these types. The basic types come already equipped with predefined operators:

```
BOOLEAN   not, or, and, implies, or else, and then
INTEGER   +, -, *, //, \\, ^, <, >, <=, >=
REAL      +, -, *, /, ^, <, >, <=, >=
```

Note The integer operator

```
//
```

represents integer division and

```
a \\ b
```

means the remainder after dividing a by b; this is the operator that is called mod or modulo in other languages.

Now one can, of course, form arbitrarily complicated **expressions** out of entities and operators:

```
a * (x + y) // ((u + v) * (u - v))
```

is such an expression.

In Chapter 3 we will deal with the expressions in more detail. Suffice it to say here that Eiffel expressions are not particularly unusual; they are formed and behave in much the same way as expressions in other Algol-like languages. We merely remark that an expression represents an anonymous object that is the result of applying the given operators in the given order to the objects bound to the given entities. Thus the expression above yields the object 3 if we have the bindings

```
a --> 2
x --> 6
y --> 7
u --> 4
v --> 3
```

An expression is a recipe for a manipulation on objects and yields another object as its result. The type of the result depends on the operator that was applied last. All the operators in our example above produce an object of type INTEGER as their result.

Note The semantics described above with the binding of entities to objects is often called 'reference semantics'. Eiffel does in fact permit a different kind of semantics called 'value semantics' or 'copy semantics'. In value semantics the test

```
x = y
```

yields true if the objects bound to x and y are equal in all their parts (attributes), although the objects may not be identical. And the assignment

```
x := y
```

means that a *copy* of the object bound to y is created and then bound to x. In particular, after this assignment the test of equality above will yield true.

Eiffel makes this alternative semantics possible by means of the so-called **expanded types**. They are not really necessary and since they make the semantics of the language vastly more complicated, we will not discuss them in this book. (The reader who does not believe expanded types make the language complicated is invited to count the number of validity rules in [Ref. 2] that have to do with expanded types.)

We saw that one can change the binding of an entity with an assignment

```
x := y
```

The reader may have wondered: 'What happens to the object that was bound to x before this assignment?' The answer depends on whether the value of x was also bound to other entities. If so, then the number of entities to which this object was bound is simply reduced by one. However, it could happen that the entity x was the only one bound to the object before the assignment. After the assignment that object is no longer bound to any entities. It can no longer be manipulated or operated upon by the program, because it has no 'handles'. It has become *garbage*. One of the tasks of the Eiffel runtime system is to 'recycle' such garbage. That is, it periodically looks for such objects that are no longer bound to any entity and returns them to the memory pool from which new objects are created. This function of the runtime system is known as *garbage collection*.

The reader may also have wondered why there was no 'destruction' instruction to correspond to the creation instruction

```
!!x
```

That would be an instruction with which one could tell the system: 'This object is no longer needed; take it back.' Such an instruction would be very dangerous; the programmer would have to be sure that there really was no other entity bound to that object before calling the destructor. Otherwise he would cause 'dangling entities' – a serious source of program errors. Such chores can be handled much better by the runtime system. The programmer should not have to worry about the recycling process. Therefore, there is no 'destructor' in Eiffel.

Chapter 3

Instructions

3.1 Making things happen

The language constructs in Eiffel that really 'compute' something are of two
kinds: **instructions** and **expressions**. The instructions cause changes in the
state of the system; they cause things to 'happen'. The expressions, on the other
hand, are combinations of entities and operators, say

    (x + y * z) / (x ^ 2 + y ^ 2 + z ^ 2)

and provide the means to compute a value. Ideally, expressions ought never to
produce any change to the state of the system, although Eiffel does not strictly
prevent them from doing so. In this chapter we mainly treat the instructions,
although expressions will often be mentioned; in Section 4.4 the expressions are
treated more fully.

Remark Many languages (particularly those that are typically interpreted
rather than compiled) do not make this distinction between 'instruction' and
'expression'. In such languages (for example Lisp or Smalltalk) every language
construct, including those that are regarded as instructions in Eiffel, returns
some kind of value.

   If we ignore the world outside the program for the moment, then the **state**
of a system consists of the set of non-garbage objects and the set of bindings
of entities to these objects. Thus we have already seen the two most basic
instructions: creation and assignment. With the creation instruction

    !!x

we generate a new object of the type of entity x and simultaneously bind x to
this new object. With the assignment instruction

    x := y

10

we alter the binding of x. Regardless of the object to which x was bound before (it could have been unbound), after the execution of the assignment above x is bound to the same object as y.

3.2 The compound instruction

All other instructions are essentially concatenations or modifications of these two basic instructions. A concatenation of instructions (a **compound instruction**) is merely a sequence

```
inst1
inst2
...
instk
```

of instructions and the meaning (semantics) is that the instructions

```
inst1, inst2, ..., instk
```

are to be executed one after the other in the given order.

One often uses semicolons to separate the individual instructions (especially if several are written on one line), but the semicolon as a separator is purely optional in Eiffel.

3.3 The conditional instruction

Often, one wants to carry out an instruction only if some condition is fulfilled. For this purpose we have the **conditional instruction**, which has the general form

```
if b1 then
    c1
elseif b2 then
    c2
...
elseif bk then
    ck
else
    ce
end
```

Here b1, b2, ... , bk are BOOLEAN expressions (i.e. expressions producing objects of type BOOLEAN as their result) and c1, c2, ..., ck, ce are compound instructions. The meaning (semantics) of this conditional instruction is intuitively clear: the BOOLEAN expressions b1, b2, ... are evaluated one after another until one is found that yields `true` – say `bj`. Then the corresponding compound instruction `cj` is executed. If none of the `BOOLEAN` expressions `b1`, `b2`, ... yields `true` upon evaluation, then the compound instruction `ce` is executed.

At this point it is appropriate to remark that the empty sequence of instructions is also a valid compound instruction whose execution does absolutely nothing (i.e. does not alter the state of the system). Thus the following is a legal conditional instruction:

```
if x < y then
    min := x
else
end
```

If the expression `x < y` yields `false`, then the conditional instruction does nothing. Since this situation is so common, one is allowed to leave out the `else` part of a conditional instruction if the corresponding compound instruction `ce` would be the empty instruction. Hence we could write the conditional instruction above as follows:

```
if x < y then
    min := x
end
```

3.4   The multibranch instruction

A variant of the conditional instruction is given by the **multibranch instruction**. It has the following form:

```
inspect exp
when s1 then
    c1
when s2 then
    c2
...
when sk then
    ck
else
    ce
end
```

The expression `exp` must be of type `INTEGER` or `CHARACTER`. It is evaluated and the result tested for membership in the sets `s1`, `s2`, ..., `sk` one after another until one is found to which the result belongs – say `sj`. Then the compound instruction `cj` is executed and the multibranch instruction is complete. If the result is in none of the sets s1, s2,..., then the compound instruction ce is executed.

In this case, too, the else clause may be omitted, but only if it is certain that the result of evaluating the expression exp will be in one of the sets s1, s2, ... sk. Unlike the situation with the conditional instruction above, here a run time error results if the result is in none of the sets s1, s2, ... sk and there is no else clause.

The sets used here may be either lists

    a1, a2, ..., an

or intervals

    a1 .. a2

of the appropriate type (i.e. the same type as exp), or a combination of both. The names a1, a2, ... appearing here must be the names of objects of the corresponding type (INTEGER or CHARACTER) or the names of constant entities. They may not be general expressions.

Example

```
inspect input_char

when 'A' .. 'Z' then
    ch_type := Upper_case

when 'a' .. 'z' then
    ch_type := Lower_case

when ',' , ';' , ':' , '.' , '?' , '!' then
    ch_type := Punctuation

else
    ch_type := Special

end
```

In the case of the type INTEGER it is clear what an interval means. With the type CHARACTER this is not so clear; what order is imposed on the objects of type CHARACTER? The language definition says that one may assume the ASCII order.

The language definition requires that the sets s1, s2, ... in a multibranch instruction must all be disjoint. Otherwise, the result of such a multibranch instruction would depend on the order of the cases.

The multibranch instruction is not strictly necessary since one could achieve the same effect with a conditional instruction – although the latter would typically be much longer. The inspect instruction is seldom used in Eiffel for reasons we shall see in Chapter 6.

3.5   The iteration instruction

Often, we must carry out a compound instruction repeatedly until some condition is fulfilled. To deal with this common situation we have the **iteration
instruction** in Eiffel. It has the following form:

```
from
    c1    -- loop initialization
until
    b     -- exit condition
loop
    c2    -- body of the loop
end
```

Here c1, c2 are compound instructions and b is a BOOLEAN expression. The
meaning of this instruction is: c1 is carried out once. Then the expression b
is evaluated. If it yields false, then c2 is executed and b is evaluated again.
This sequence of operations is repeated until eventually the evaluation of b yields
true. Then the iteration instruction is complete.

Incidentally, we see here the form of comments in Eiffel. They are introduced
by the double dash -- and extend to the end of the line.

The experienced programmer may ask 'How does one leave the loop prema-
turely when some special condition makes this necessary?' The answer is that
this is not possible in Eiffel. Such premature exits from loops often make the
proof of correctness of loops very difficult. For that reason it was decided not to
include premature exits in Eiffel.

3.6   The debug instruction

The debug instruction has the form

```
debug ( key1, ..., keyn )
    c
end
```

where c is an arbitrary compound instruction. When debugging is turned on,
the compound instruction c is executed whenever control reaches the debug
instruction. When debugging is turned off, the **debug** instruction has no effect.

Debugging can be turned on selectively by using *keys*. If debugging is turned
on for one of the keys listed in the above **debug** instruction, then this instruction
is activated. The keys are arbitrary strings.

3.7   Procedures and functions

We have now seen almost all the kinds of instructions provided by the language.
The programmer, however, can construct instructions for her own purposes –

custom-made instructions, so to speak. These are the **procedures**. Syntactically a procedure is defined as follows:

```
pname (arg1 : T1; arg2 : T2; ...; argn : Tn) is

    local
                -- here the declaration of
                -- local entities

    do
          c       -- compound instruction; the body
    end
```

The do and the end are obligatory (although in the deferred and external routines that we encounter later the do will be replaced by other reserved words). The local clause is optional. The compound instruction c can, at least in theory, be an empty instruction (then the procedure is a so-called 'stub'; it does nothing).

pname is the name given to the procedure being defined here; it will be used whenever we want to execute the newly defined instruction. Here arg1, arg2, ..., argn are the names of local entities called **formal arguments** of the procedure pname. The types of these entities are T1, T2, ..., Tn.

Remark The list of formal arguments is one of the two constructs where the language definition makes a semicolon obligatory. Groups of arguments of different types must be separated by semicolons. The requirement is quite arbitrary and this author, for one, would have been very happy to be freed from the pestiferous semicolon under which so many Pascal programmers have suffered.

Further local entities may be declared in the local clause. These local entities may be used anywhere in the compound instruction c where entities may be used, that is, in expressions or as the targets of assignments. The formal arguments can also be used in any expression occuring in the procedure. They may not, however, be the target (left-hand side) of an assignment. A further distinction between the formal arguments and the other local entities will be explained shortly.

Here we have, in effect, put some wrapping around the compound instruction c and given it a (hopefully suggestive) name. We can now execute this instruction anywhere where the other kinds of instruction can be executed. In an Eiffel text we do so by including a line of the form

```
pname (e1, e2, ..., en)
```

Here e1, e2, ..., en are expressions – ei of type Ti, $1 <= i <= n$ – and are called the **actual arguments**. One usually says 'the procedure pname is *called* with arguments e1, e2, ...'. The meaning (semantics) of such a 'call' is as follows. The actual arguments e1, e2, ... are evaluated. For each i the formal argument argi is bound to the result of evaluating ei. The local entities declared in the local clause are bound to the appropriate default objects. Then the compound instruction c is executed.

If it weren't for the arguments and the local entities this would have just the same effect as if one were to replace every reference to pname by the compound instruction c.

We have seen that the formal arguments and the local entities declared in the local clause are treated very similarly inside the procedure. The difference is merely that the formal arguments are 'initialized' by the caller of the procedure, who provides the actual arguments. The local entities, on the other hand, are 'initialized' with default objects.

There is, however, one other difference that is laid down by the language definition: one is not allowed to assign to formal arguments in the body of the procedure. Such an assignment would have no effect anyway, since the formal arguments are not 'visible' outside of the procedure; that is, these entities effectively do not exist except in the context of the procedure. Thus what is bound to them is irrelevant when the procedure is finished. We mention the stricture against assigning to formal arguments only because it will lead to an error message from the compiler if ignored.

Functions are in many ways quite analogous to procedures. Just as a procedure is a custom-made instruction created by packaging a compound instruction, so a function is generally a packaged expression. The function provides a suggestive name for the expression and is responsible for returning the value of the expression to the caller. A function returns a value and so the text giving the definition of a function must specify the type of the value (object) returned. This is almost the only syntactical difference between functions and procedures. Here is the general form of a function definition:

```
fname (arg1 : T1; arg2 : T2; ...; argn : Tn) : T is

    local
                -- here the declaration of
                -- local entities

    do
        c       -- compound instruction; the body

    end
```

We have declared here that the function will return an object of type T as its value.

However, there must be some mechanism by which the body of the function specifies the value to be returned. This is achieved by including an assignment instruction of the form

```
result := expression
```

in the body of the function. The predeclared local entity `result` may only be used in functions and the value it receives in the last such assignment carried out in the function body determines the value of the function itself. There may be arbitrarily many such assignments to `result` in the body of the function (including 0; in this case the returned value is the default value of type T).

Let us look at an example of an Eiffel routine:

```
square (x : REAL) : REAL is

    do
        result := x * x
    end
```

Here we define a routine and give it the name `square`. In this simple example the body of the routine consists of a single instruction

```
result := x * x
```

The routine `square` is a function; it computes a result – in this case a real number. The new function `square` has one argument of type REAL to which we give the inspired name `x`.

The new routine `square` can be used as if it were a further primitive operation. The value of the expression `square (3.0)` is of course 9.0 and the expression `square (3.0)` may appear anywhere where the expression 9.0 would be acceptable. We can use our new routine to define further (more complex) routines:

```
sum_of_squares (x, y : REAL) : REAL is

    do
        result := square (x) + square (y)
    end
```

Now let us look at a less trivial example. How does one compute the greatest common divisor of two integers m, n? One can of course try all integers q which are smaller than

$$p = min(m, n)$$

and take the largest one that divides both m and n. This method would require approximately $2p$ divisions and many comparisons (if `r < s then` ...). However, already in 300 B.C. Euclid knew of a better method, which today is known as 'Euclid's algorithm'. The essential observation is that if r is the remainder after dividing m by n, then

$$gcd(m, n) = gcd(n, r) \text{ and } r < n$$

So we can reduce the problem to computing the gcd for smaller numbers and we can repeat this reduction until, finally, one of the numbers becomes 0. Here is the solution as an Eiffel routine:

```
gcd (m, n : INTEGER) : INTEGER  is
            -- m, n non-negative!

do
    if n = 0 then
        result := m
    else
        result := gcd (n, m \\ n)
    end
end
```

Remarks

- The function **gcd** is defined by calling itself. This kind of self-reference is known as recursion. Recursion is permitted and indeed is very useful in Eiffel.
- The result of **gcd** is not likely to be correct if one or both of the arguments is negative. For this reason we have written the comment

```
-- m, n non-negative!
```

at the beginning of the function definition. We will see a better method of formulating such restrictions in Chapter 5.

The greatest common divisor can also be computed without using recursion, but the solution is somewhat longer:

```
gcd (m, n : INTEGER) : INTEGER is

local
    other, remain : INTEGER

do
    from
        result := m
        remain := n
    until
        remain = 0
    loop
        other  := result
        result := remain
        remain := other \\ result
    end
end
```

Important Remark We stated earlier that the role of expressions and functions is to compute a value, not to change the state of the system. Changing the state of the system is the task of instructions. However, there is nothing in the Eiffel language definition to prevent one from including state-altering instructions in the body of a function. Such a function is said to have **side effects**. Functions with side effects make it much more difficult to demonstrate the correctness of a program. Therefore, we should make every effort to write functions that have no side effects. We will mention this resolution occasionally in the following chapters.

3.8 External routines

At the beginning of this chapter we used the phrase 'If we ignore the world outside the program for the moment ...'. Up until now we have been busy ignoring the outside world. But of course one cannot always do so. A program must somehow communicate with the outer world – be it only to find out what the user wants done. In practice this means communicating with the operating system (which in turn communicates with the user). So there must be an interface between an Eiffel program and the operating system.

This interface will consist of certain procedures and functions that are not part of the Eiffel program and as a rule are not written in Eiffel. But Eiffel provides a way of making such routines appear as if they were part of the Eiffel system. They are declared as **external** routines using a declaration of the following sort:

```
pname (arg1 : T1; arg2 : T2; ...; argn : Tn) is

    external "C"
    alias "other_name"

    end
```

This declaration describes a procedure which in the rest of the Eiffel program looks just like an Eiffel procedure and can be used (i.e. called) just like an Eiffel procedure. But the **external** clause tells the Eiffel compiler not to look for or compile any Eiffel code for this procedure. It is external to the Eiffel system and in this case is written in the language C. (At the time of writing, C is the only external language supported by existing implementations.)

Example A procedure for sending a string to the terminal could thus be declared as follows:

```
put_string (text : STRING) is

    external "C"
    alias "C_string_put"
    end
```

The `alias` clause is provided so that one is not forced to give an external procedure the same name inside the Eiffel system that it has outside. This is not only practical but in fact necessary because Eiffel is case insensitive; a name written in upper case is identical to the same name written in lower case. But C is case sensitive; it makes a difference which case is used. Moreover, identifier names in C are allowed to begin with an underline character; in Eiffel this is not permitted.

External functions are declared using the following syntax:

```
fname (arg1 : T1; arg2 : T2; ...; argn : Tn) : T is


    external "C"
    alias "other_name"


    end
```

3.9   Exercises

1. Program an Eiffel function

    ```
    power (base : REAL, exp : INTEGER) : REAL
    ```

    that computes **base** raised to the power **exp**. Your solution should not use the operator ^ and should require approximately

    $$2 \log_2(|exp|)$$

    multiplications. Try giving both an iterative and a recursive solution.

2. Write a function

    ```
    change (amount : INTEGER) : INTEGER
    ```

    that computes in how many ways a given amount of money (in pennies) can be represented using the coins penny, nickel, dime, quarter and half-dollar (or some other denominations suitable for your country).

    Hint: The problem is fairly simple if you let **change** call a function

    ```
    how_many_ways (amount, kinds : INTEGER) : INTEGER
    ```

    that has as arguments the amount to be changed and the number of kinds of coins that may be used. For example, **kinds = 3** would mean that only pennies, nickels and dimes are allowed. This function, in turn, can be programmed as a recursive function if one observes that the answer required is the sum of the ways to change **amount** using (**kinds - 1**) kinds of coins plus the ways to change **amount - max** using **kinds** sorts of coins. Here **max** means the value of the largest kind of coin allowed. The only ticklish part is making sure you deal with the 'boundary' cases properly.

Chapter 4

Classes and Objects

4.1 Classification

In trying to understand the world around us we find it helpful to classify the objects we can distinguish in the physical world or in our mental world into **classes**. A class consists of all objects with similar properties and similar behavior: the class of all vicious dogs, the class of all procedural languages, etc. In Eiffel, as in all object-oriented languages, we also sort our data objects into classes. Actually, as Bertrand Meyer has often remarked, the denomination 'object-oriented' for languages like Eiffel is a misnomer; 'class-oriented' would describe them much better.

In real life it is often difficult to specify exactly what we mean by 'similar properties' and 'similar behavior'. With programming languages things are fortunately much simpler. In Eiffel the *properties* of an object will be given by a list of entities of varying types that belong to the object; they are called the **attributes** of the object. The *behavior* of an object will be defined by a list of **routines** (procedures and functions) that belong to the object. (In talking about Eiffel one uses the term 'routine' to subsume both functions and procedures.)

If two objects belong to the same class, then their attributes will have the same names and types. Their routines will also be identical. The attributes and routines together form the **features** of the object.

In Eiffel, one does not write programs; one writes classes. The text of an Eiffel class describes the features (i.e. the attributes and routines) of every object belonging to the class. Thus one could think of the class text as being a pattern for the generation of arbitrarily many objects of the given class. The objects generated from a class description are call **instances** of the class. The class text has the following form:

```
class CNAME

creation
        -- here the name(s) of the
        -- creation procedure(s)

feature
            -- here the declaration or
            -- definition of all features

end -- class CNAME
```

The `feature` clause will contain declarations of the attributes (entities) and definitions of the routines belonging to objects of this class.

The `creation` clause is optional. If it is present it names one or more procedures appearing in the `feature` clause. One of these creation procedures must be called every time an object of the given class is created. The job of a creation procedure is to initialize the object, i.e. to give its attributes sensible values. To this end the creation instruction, with which we became acquainted in Chapter 2, has an extended syntax:

```
    !!x.create_proc (e1, e2, ...)
```

Here `create_proc` is one of the creation procedures given in the class of `x`. It is called immediately after creation of the object bound to `x`. Creation procedures may of course have formal arguments just as other procedures do. In that case actual arguments `e1, e2, ...` of appropriate types must be given when calling the creation procedure. These are typically appropriate initial values for some of the attributes.

The type and class of an object are in fact one and the same thing; for objects the terms 'class' and 'type' are synonymous. Later when we encounter the generic classes (Chapter 8) it will at first appear that they break this rule; however, we shall not regard generic classes as actual classes. Thus it is correct to say that the name of a type is the name of a class. Or, put another way, specifying the type of an entity specifies the class of objects to which this entity may be bound.

4.2   Abstract data types

In Eiffel, classes are typically used to implement abstract data types (ADTs). An abstract data type is one that is defined by its interface to the rest of the system and not by its implementation. In other words, an abstract data type is described by *what* it can do for its user and not by *how* it does it.

We can illustrate this idea with the example of the ADT LIST. Our ADT LIST will provide the following operations:

```
add (x : ELEMENT)      -- Add 'x' to the list.
remove (x : ELEMENT) -- Remove 'x' from the list.
```

In addition, it provides the following 'functions', which might actually be attributes in a given implementation:

```
has (x : ELEMENT) : BOOLEAN -- Is 'x' in the list?
count : INTEGER             -- How many elements does
                            -- the list have?
empty : BOOLEAN             -- Is the list empty?
```

The following axioms are to hold between these procedures and functions:

1. After add (x) we have has (x).
2. After remove (x) we have not has (x).
3. empty is true precisely if count = 0.
4. If not has (x), then after add (x) we have count = old count + 1.
5. If has (x), then after remove (x) we have count = old count - 1.

Remarks

1. From Axiom 2 it follows that an element can be in the list at most once, i.e.

   ```
   add (x)
   add (x)
   ```

   has the same effect as a single add (x). We could of course implement lists that allowed duplicates but then the axioms would be somewhat more complicated.
2. The type ELEMENT actually stands for a quite arbitrary type – simply the type of the objects to be stored in the list. As we will soon see, the implementation of the list is completely independent of what this type might be. Thus it is annoying that we need this type at all. However, the formal arguments of add, remove and has are required to have types. In Chapter 8 we will see how to get rid of this crutch once we have introduced the generic classes.

We are going to implement our lists as so-called 'linked lists'. This is not the most efficient solution but it is comparatively easy to understand. The idea is to use **nodes** that are chained together like pearls in a necklace as illustrated in Fig. 4.1. Each node has two attributes: 'its' element and its right neighbor. The corresponding class NODE is very simple:

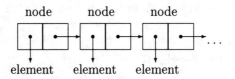

Figure 4.1 A linked list

```
class NODE

feature

    item : ELEMENT
    next : NODE

-----------------------------------------------------------

    set_item (x : ELEMENT) is

        do
            item := x
        end
-----------------------------------------------------------

    set_next (n : NODE) is

        do
            next := n
        end

end -- class NODE
```

Armed with this raw material we can now easily build our lists. An object of type LIST only needs to remember two things:

- the first node in the list (attribute **first**),
- the number of nodes or elements (attribute **count**).

The following is our class LIST:

```
class LIST

feature

    count : INTEGER
    first : NODE
----------------------------------------------------------

    empty : BOOLEAN is

        do
            result := (count = 0)
        end
----------------------------------------------------------

    has (x : ELEMENT) : BOOLEAN is

        local
            n : NODE
        do
            from
                n := first
            until
                n = void or else equal (x, n.item)
            loop
                n := n.next
            end

            result := (n /= void)
        end
----------------------------------------------------------

    add (x : ELEMENT) is

        local
            n : NODE
        do
            if not has (x) then
                !!n
                n.set_item (x)
                n.set_next (first)
                first := n
                count := count + 1
            end
        end
```

```
    remove (x : ELEMENT) is

        local
            pre, post : NODE

        do
            from
                pre := first
            until
                pre = void or else equal (x, pre.item)
            loop
                post := pre
                pre  := pre.next
            end

            if pre /= void then        -- found it!
                if first = void then -- was 1st node
                    first := pre.next
                else
                    post.set_next (pre.next)
                end

                count := count - 1
            end
        end

end -- class LIST
```

The above relatively simple example illustrates several aspects of programming with Eiffel. The function **has** is very simple; with the local entity n of type NODE we walk along the list from node to node until we either reach the end (n = void) or find the element we are looking for (equal (x, n.item)). But what is the function **equal** (obviously of type BOOLEAN)? It is a predefined function available in every class. It has the apparently surprising property that its arguments can be of an arbitrary type (as with the operators =, /=). It returns **true** as result when

- both arguments are of the same type and
- both arguments are equal attribute for attribute (in the sense of =).

Hence the test equal (x,y) is not the same thing as the test x = y, as Fig. 4.2 illustrates. In this figure we have three different objects N1, N2, N3 of type NODE. If the entities n_1, n_2, n_3 are bound to N1, N2 and N3, then we have

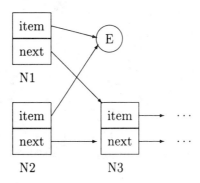

Figure 4.2 The notion of equality

n_1 /= n_2. But here the expression equal (n_1, n_2) will yield true. The
item attributes agree (both have the value E) and the next attributes agree (both
have the value N3).

One should remark at this point that the equality tests = and equal agree on
the basic types BOOLEAN, CHARACTER, INTEGER, REAL and DOUBLE. Objects of the
basic types have no attributes, so objects of these types can only be equal in the
sense of equal if they are the same object.

The question of what 'equality' means is quite generally a ticklish question
and in no way a special problem of Eiffel. For this reason many programming
languages have several different sorts of test for equality.

We could, of course, have implemented our class LIST in such a way that has
and remove used = rather than equal. Then the semantics of our lists would
have been different. The reader should be sure that she understands what the
differences would be and what the advantages and disadvantages of the two
possible implementations are.

Our procedure add is also very simple. It first uses has to determine whether
the element x is already in the list. Only if it is not yet there is it added. If we
had decided to allow duplicates this test would of course have been unnecessary.
If x is not yet in the list, then a new node is created (!!n) and x is made to be
the item of this node. Then the new node is prepended to the list. After this
move first points to the new node. Fig. 4.3 illustrates this operation.

The routine remove is a little more complicated. Here we need two local
entities pre and post that march through the list one after the other. In case
we find the element x with pre, the entity post will be bound to the predecessor
node of the one holding x. (post remains void if x is the first element in the
list.) With the instruction

```
post.set_next (pre.next)
```

the successor of the node pre is made to be the new successor of post. Then
the node pre is effectively disconnected from the list. The removal operation is

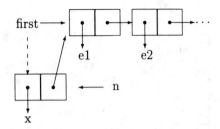

Figure 4.3 Adding to a linked list

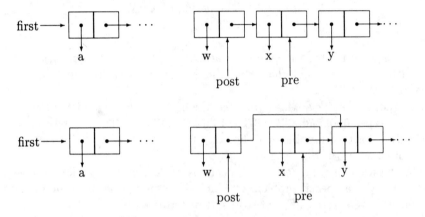

Figure 4.4 Removing from a list

illustrated by Fig. 4.4.

The reader may be surprised that no steps are taken here to eliminate the now superfluous node containing **x**. But remember that this sort of task is the job of the garbage collector in Eiffel.

Our class LIST has the attribute **count** and the routines **empty**, **has**, **add** and **remove**. These are the features that ought to belong to the interface according to the definition of the abstract data type LIST. But the class also needs some other features in order to be able to remember which elements are currently in the LIST; in our implementation this is the attribute **first**. This feature definitely belongs to the category 'implementation' and ought not to be visible in the interface. As things stand so far, however, it would be just as available to the user of the class LIST as the other features. To solve this problem Eiffel offers the ability to **export** some features and hide others.

There may be arbitrarily many **feature** clauses in a class definition and the **feature** clause may be qualified by a list of classes to which the features are to be exported:

```
feature { C1, C2, ..., Ck }
```

This qualification means that all features between this **feature** clause and the next one (or the end of the class text) are exported only to the classes C1, C2, ..., Ck. The statement 'feature f is exported to class C' means that objects in class C may use the the feature f. For example, if f is a procedure, then objects of class C may call this procedure f in their routines.

If the **feature** clause is not qualified by a list of classes, then the features following it are exported to all classes. An equivalent way of formulating this is to write

```
feature { ANY }
```

There is also a way to make a feature invisible outside of its own class. One writes

```
feature { NONE }
```

to achieve this restriction. In fact, this restriction is even stronger than it might at first appear: attributes following the above clause will not even be available to other objects of the same class. They may only be accessed by the object to which they belong – they are strictly private. If one wants to let other objects of the same class (say A) access a feature, then one must allow this by saying explicitly

```
feature { A }
```

We may now alter our implementation of the ADT LIST as follows:

```
class LIST

feature

    -- count, empty, has, add, remove as above

feature { NONE }

    first : NODE [ELEMENT]

end -- class LIST
```

This is the principle of **information hiding**. Everything not belonging to the advertised interface is invisible outside the class.

4.3   Accessing features of an object

We said earlier that the attributes of an object represent its properties and its routines represent its behavior. But how do we make use of these properties and this behavior? What we really mean by this question is: how can one object ask another about its state or ask it to carry out one of its advertised operations? Let us consider the typical situation where this need will arise.

Let B, C be two classes and suppose that C has an entity of type B:

```
x : B
```

In this situation one says that C is a **client** of B and B is a **supplier** of C.

Suppose, further, that B has an attribute a of type D and a procedure p. Then a routine in the class C might need the value of attribute a of the object bound to its entity x. It can attain this value with the expression

```
x : B
y : D

  . . .

y := x.a
```

And it can call the procedure p of the object bound to x by executing the instruction

```
x.p
```

One thinks of this notation as meaning: the value of x is asked to report the value of a or to execute its procedure p. In the object-oriented language Smalltalk one would say: 'one sends a message to x asking for the value of a or asking it to execute p'.

If the procedure p has s formal arguments, then the call would look as follows:

```
x.p (e1, e2, ..., es)
```

where e1, e2, ..., es are s expressions of the appropriate types.

In the same way one can ask for the value of a function f of the class B having s formal arguments and returning a result of type D by using an expression such as

```
y : D

  . . .

y := x.f (e1, e2, ..., es)
```

The object bound to x is asked to evaluate its function f with actual arguments e1, e2, ..., es and to send back the result.

Remark If f is a function without any formal arguments, then the expression x.f for evaluating f looks just the same as it would if f were an attribute of the same type instead. Thus the user of the class B cannot tell from the outside whether f is an attribute or a function without arguments. This ambiguity is quite intentional; the user should not have to know or care which it is, since the effect is the same in both cases. This ambiguity then gives the implementor of the class B the freedom to make f an attribute or a function, whichever seems most expedient to her. She could even alter her decision at some later time without affecting the users of her class B in any way.

Very Important Remark

If an entity x is not bound to any object (i.e. x = void), then clearly there is no point asking the object bound to x to return the value of an attribute or to execute a routine. This is reflected in Eiffel by the fact that it is a runtime error to evaluate x.a or x.f or x.f (e1, e2, ...) if x = void.

Another Important Remark

It is not possible in Eiffel for one object to alter the attributes of another object by means of assignment – say by such an instruction as the following:

```
x.a := u
```

If such manipulation were allowed, the object bound to x would have no way of guaranteeing that it fulfills the axioms of the abstract data type it implements, for it could never know what others were doing to it by 'remote manipulation'. The only one allowed to alter the attributes of an object is the object itself. It must be asked to do so by calling a suitable procedure of the class. Thus some classes may have many procedures of the following type:

```
set_a (new_a : T) is

    do
        if is_valid (new_a) then
            a := new_a
        end
    end
```

Meyer uses the following metaphor: an object is a machine with some meters and buttons. The attributes and functions are the meters and these provide information about the internal state of the machine. The procedures are the buttons and can be used to alter the state of the machine in a controlled way.

Sometimes a routine needs to refer to the object for which the routine was called, the object for which it is currently executing. It may do so with the predefined entity `current`. In other object-oriented languages this entity is called `this` (C++) or `self` (Smalltalk).

When the routine of an object refers to the object's own attributes it simply uses the name of the corresponding entity without the dot notation. Thus an attribute with name `a` is referred to simply as `a`. This is equivalent to referring to

    current.a

In fact, `current` is the first formal argument of every routine of the class and has the type of the class itself. When the routine is called, `current` is bound to the object which was asked to carry out the routine.

The formal argument `current` is not mentioned in the list of formal arguments because it is always the same; it would be tiresome and redundant always to have to include it.

Example   The feature call

    x. f(u, v)

leads to the formal argument `current` of `f` being bound to the same object to which `x` is bound.

4.4   Expressions

We return once more to the expressions that were mentioned frequently in preceding chapters. Now that we have learned about classes we can explain more thoroughly what expressions are. This section could be very short, for in theory every Eiffel expression of type `B` occurring in the class text of a class `A` is in one of the following forms:

```
        x        -- a simple expression of type B
or      e.x      -- e an expression of type C and x a simple
                 -- expression of type B occuring in class C
```

In turn, a simple expression in a class `A` has one of the following forms:

```
        a                  -- an attribute of A
or      f                  -- a function of A without arguments
or      f (e1, e2, ...) -- "      "     "  " with          "
```

The expressions `e1, e2, ...`, which are the actual arguments of `f`, must of course have the same types as the formal arguments of `f` (more precisely: they must conform to the formal arguments).

Expressions are evaluated from left to right. Thus the expression

    x.f (y, z).g (u, v, w).h (3, 4)

is evaluated as follows:

1. The value of x is determined. Let it be an object O1.
2. Then the values of y and z are determined; let these be objects O2 and O3. The object O1 is asked to evaluate its function f with actual arguments O2, O3. Let the result be an object O4.
3. Now the values of u, v and w are determined; let these be objects O5, O6 and O7. Object O4 is asked to evaluate its function g with actual arguments O5, O6 and O7. Let the result be an object O8.
4. Finally, object O8 is asked to evaluate its function h with arguments 3 and 4. The result of this evaluation is an object O9 and is the value of the entire expression.

This would be almost all there is to say about Eiffel expressions if it were not for the fact that Eiffel permits one to use the more traditional **infix notation** for functions of one argument (actually two arguments; remember **current!**). Thus instead of writing

    x.f (y)

one may declare f to be an `infix` operator and then write

    x f y

for the same expression.

The operators

    +, -, *, ^, /, //, \\, <, >, <=, >=

in the basic classes as well as `or`, `or else`, `and`, `and then`, `implies` in `BOOLEAN` are all `infix` operators. If one did not have this possibility one would have to write the expression

    (x - y) / (u + v)

instead as

    x.- (y)./ (u.+ (v))

Now the infix operators are notorious for the parenthesizing problems that they raise. If one does not fully parenthesize every complex expression, then **precedence rules** are needed to clear up ambiguities.

Example Does the expression

   $a + b * c$

mean

   $(a + b) * c$ or $a + (b * c)$?

One would normally expect it to mean the latter. In programming languages this is settled by specifying that the multiplication operator * takes precedence over the addition operator +. One also says '* binds more tightly than +'.

In Eiffel we have this problem with the infix operators just as in every other language. Thus we specify the precedence levels of operators to be the following.

Level	Operator
10	.
9	old, not, unary +, unary -, free unary operators
8	free binary operators
7	^
6	*, /, //, \\
5	+, -
4	=, /=, <, >, <=, >=
3	and, and then
2	or, or else
1	implies

This is to be interpreted as follows: if operator a appears higher in the list than operator b, then a takes precedence over or binds tighter than b. Operators at the same level have equal precedence.

Example   Since + and - are at the same precedence level, it is not clear whether the expression

$$a + b - c$$

is to be interpreted as

$$(a + b) - c \quad \text{or as} \quad a + (b - c)$$

The rule here is that such expressions are evaluated from left to right. Thus $(a + b) - c$ is the right interpretation.

Remark   The two predefined operators **and then** and **or else** in the class **BOOLEAN** are an exception to the general pattern. These two operators use *lazy evaluation* of their arguments. That means the following. To evaluate the expression

```
e1 and then e2
```

the Eiffel system first evaluates the expression e1. If it is **false** then the value of the entire expression is **false** and the expression e2 is never evaluated. If, however, e1 evaluates to **true**, then e2 is also evaluated and the result of the entire expression is the value of e2.

Similarly, the expression

```
e1 or else e2
```

is evaluated by first evaluating `e1`. If the value is **true**, then the value of the entire expression is **true** and `e2` is never evaluated. If, however, `e1` evaluates to **false**, then `e2` is evaluted and its value becomes the value of the entire expression.

This kind of lazy evaluation can be very important in such expressions as

```
if x /= void and then x.count > 0 then
    . . .
```

or

```
if x = void or else x.count = 0 then
    . . .
```

since evaluating `x.count` when `x` is **void** will lead to a runtime error.

A function of one argument (or two, if you count **current**) may be declared to be an infix operator by qualifying its definition with the reserved word **infix**. The names of such operators are formed out of the non-alphanumeric characters

```
@, #, &, |, +, -, *, /, ^, <, >
```

and must be quoted in the definition of the operator. The operators +, -, *, /, ^, < and > are 'standard' operators provided by the language. In addition, a programmer may define so-called 'free' operators, whose names can be any string not containing a blank and beginning with one of the following symbols:

```
@, #, &, |
```

4.5   Constants

It is possible to declare attributes as *read-only*, that is, as constant attributes. The syntax for such declarations is as follows:

```
max_size : INTEGER is 4096
pi       : REAL is 3.14159
warning  : STRING is "Watch out!"
vector   : ARRAY [INTEGER] is <<3, 4, 5, -2, 7>>
```

In fact these 'declarations' are really definitions just as with procedures and functions (one recognizes definitions by the reserved word **is**). The object to be bound to the declared (or, rather, defined) entity is found to the right of the word **is**. Such constant declarations are only possible for those types whose objects may have predefined names.

We already knew that the objects of basic type **BOOLEAN**, **CHARACTER**, **INTEGER** and **REAL** had predefined names. We now see that the non-basic but special types **STRING** and **ARRAY** also have this property. Objects of type **STRING** can be described with a *literal string* enclosed in quotation marks, as in the example "Watch out!" above. In the same way, array objects can be described by *manifest arrays* enclosed in double pointed brackets <<...>>, as in the example above.

Just as the names of routines may not appear as the target of an assignment, so, too, read-only entities (constants) may not be the target of an assignment.

Of course, a literal string or a manifest array may occur in any expression in which a string or an array is expected. In particular this is true of the actual arguments in a routine call.

Examples

If the procedure p is declared as follows

```
p (a : ARRAY [INTEGER]) is ...
```

then it is permissible to call p using

```
p (<<3, 56, -123, 44>>)
```

or also

```
p (<<x, y, z>>)
```

where x, y and z are expressions of type INTEGER.

In just the same way we may use literal strings as arguments to routine calls:

```
io.putstring ("Hello, world!%N")
```

There are some situations where the programmer does not care what value a read-only attribute has; the only important thing is that different attributes have different values. For this situation Eiffel provides the reserved word **unique**:

```
red    : INTEGER is unique
blue   : INTEGER is unique
green  : INTEGER is unique
black  : INTEGER is unique
```

Here the programmer is telling the compiler to assign the values according to some suitable scheme and make sure they are all different. What the actual values are does not interest the programmer. She will probably use them in a multibranch instruction such as the following:

```
inspect color

when red then
    ...
when blue
    ...
when green
    ...
```

Note

The values assigned by the unique mechanism are only guaranteed to be unique *within the enclosing class*. Values assigned using unique in different classes may in fact overlap.

The language definition does guarantee that the values assigned by unique will all be positive. Thus the programmer may use negative values or zero and be sure that they will not conflict with the unique values.

Eiffel also provides something like 'constant routines'. These are the so-called once routines. There are in fact situations in which one wants a routine to be carried out only once per program execution. A good example is an initialization procedure which may have harmful effects if carried out more than once.

In traditional systems one would prevent the repeated execution of such a procedure by introducing a global flag – say initialized – which is set by the initialization procedure. The initialization procedure checks this flag and does nothing if the flag is already set.

In Eiffel the matter is much simpler. One simply makes such an initialization procedure into a once procedure as follows:

```
init is

    once
        . . .
    end
```

The reserved word once replaces the usual do in the procedure and signals that this procedure is to be executed at most one time per program execution. Now it is quite harmless to call the procedure init at any place where one is not sure that the initialization has been carried out.

It also makes perfectly good sense to have once functions. These are essentially *computed constants*. In the function

```
f (x : T) : U is

    once
        . . .
        result := ...
    end
```

the calculation in the body of f is carried out only the first time the function is called. The runtime system remembers the result. Every successive call to f will simply return the value computed the first time – regardless of the value of the actual argument and regardless of the object for which the function is called.

4.6   Eiffel programs

We said at the outset of the chapter that one does not write programs in Eiffel; one writes classes. There is in fact no textual element more comprehensive than the class. In particular, there is nothing called 'program'. How then does one create a program, something one can 'run'?

The answer is in fact very simple. One designates a class as **root class** and singles out one of the creation procedures of this class (this is done in a special file that is read by the compiler). The compiler then produces an executable program (assuming there were no errors in the class text!). The startup code of this program creates one instance of the root class and calls the specified creation procedure of this object.

The creation procedure will typically create objects of other classes and call some of their routines. These routines do the job that the program is supposed to carry out. When the end of the creation procedure of the root object is reached, the program terminates.

This is in fact not very different from how one creates a program in C. Every C program must have a `main` function. This `main` function is called by the startup code of the C program. When the end of the `main` function is reached, the program terminates.

It follows that any Eiffel class which has at least one creation procedure could be the root class of an Eiffel program. However, one usually creates classes that are specifically intended to be root classes. The creation procedure of such a root class generally finds out what the user wants done by examining the command line with which the program was called and the environment variables defined with the help of the operating system. Then the creation procedure creates objects of various other classes and calls their routines to do its task.

4.7   Exercises

1. (a) Program a class `RATIONAL` representing the rational numbers (fractions). It should have attributes `numerator` and `denominator` as well as the usual arithmetic operations +, -, * and /. Furthermore, it needs the comparison operators <, >, <= and >= .

   (b) Do your objects of type `RATIONAL` show the expected behavior when compared using `equal`, i.e. do such fractions as $\frac{2}{3}$ and $\frac{4}{6}$ turn out to be equal? If not, how should you change your class to make this work properly?

2. Explain what difference it would make to test for equality using = instead of `equal` in the routines `has` and `remove` in the class LIST. What are the advantages or disadvantages of using the one or the other kind of test?

3. Using the ADT LIST and our Eiffel implementation with the class LIST as a starting point, implement an ADT SET having the following features:

   ```
   count : INTEGER
   empty : BOOLEAN
   add (x : ELEMENT)
   remove (x : ELEMENT)
   ```

```
has (x : ELEMENT) : BOOLEAN
infix "+" (other : SET) : SET -- union
infix "-" (other : SET) : SET -- difference
infix "*" (other : SET) : SET -- intersection
```

and the obvious axioms. For testing your class you will find it useful to have the following features as well:

```
first              -- Set 'cursor' on 1st element.
forth              -- "     "     " next element.
item : ELEMENT     -- Element 'cursor' is on.
finished : BOOLEAN -- Have we seen them all?
```

Then one can display the contents of a set with a loop such as the following:

```
io : BASIC_IO

from
    !!io
    s.first
until
    s.finished
loop
    io.put_int (s.item)
    io.put_newline
    s.forth
end
```

(where we assume that ELEMENT is INTEGER.)

Build a suitable root class for testing your class SET interactively. For this you will need to investigate the standard library class BASIC_IO if you have Eiffel/S or the corresponding input/output class in some other Eiffel implementation.

4. Write a class QUEUE implementing the abstract data type QUEUE with operations

```
add (x : ELEMENT)   -- Element 'x' arrives and
                    -- joins the queue at the end.
remove              -- The element at the front
                    -- of the queue is removed.
front : ELEMENT     -- The element at the front.
empty : BOOLEAN     -- Is the queue empty?
```

Your objects of class QUEUE should display the usual 'first-in-first-out' behavior expected of queues.

Again you will need an appropriate root class for testing your queues interactively.

Chapter 5

Correct Programs

5.1 Assertions

An incorrect program is obviously not worth much. On the other hand, everyone who has ever programmed knows how difficult it is to write absolutely error-free programs. For this reason any support that the programming environment can give in producing correct programs is extremely welcome.

We are not talking here about syntactical errors: a forgotten comma or the reserved word `elseif` inadvertently written `elsif`. Every Eiffel compiler easily finds mistakes of this kind and reports them to the programmmer so that he can repair them. In this chapter we want to assume that our programs are syntactically correct. The really difficult errors are the logical ones; the program simply does not do what we intended it to. Many of these errors make themselves evident immediately – often in the first trial run. Others, though, are much more subtle and long remain undiscovered. These latter ones are the really dangerous errors.

It would be ideal if one could prove the correctness of a program the way one proves a mathematical theorem. Naturally, we would want the proofs to be constructed automatically by some sort of tool, since it would probably be impossible, and at any rate extremely tedious, to produce by hand a proof of correctness for a longish program. Much research has been done on automatic proofs for computer programs, but most of the sucessful work in this direction is applicable only to the so-called 'functional' languages. Those are languages that (like mathematics) allow only expressions and no instructions, only functions and no procedures. With languages like Eiffel that permit assignments, the hope of achieving such proofs is very small indeed. Nevertheless, the Eiffel language does provide some very important support toward producing correct programs.

One kind of help in achieving correctness is already familiar to us: strong typing. Every entity has a type that must be declared by the programmer. This allows the compiler to determine whether a qualified routine call is correct, that is, whether the corresponding class has such a routine. This can be determined without executing the program, merely by examining the Eiffel text. Thus one of the most common sources of errors is eliminated.

When is a class correct? Precisely when each of the routines in the class does exactly what it is supposed to do and nothing more. But how can we describe what a routine should do? Of course, we can always do this with natural language, but natural languages have the disadvantage of being ambiguous or 'fuzzy'. Hence descriptions with natural language will scarcely permit an automatic verification of correctness. We need a formal means for describing what a routine should do so that an automatic check of correctness can be carried out either by inspecting the text or else while the program is running.

An exact description of a function ought to specify what value the function will compute for every possible state that the system could be in when the function is called. An exact description of a procedure ought to specify what state changes will be caused by the procedure given a complete description of the state prior to the procedure call. This characterization of a complete specification should make it clear to the reader that such specifications are unpracticable in most cases. The Eiffel text of a routine is often the most compact and most precise description of the routine that one can give.

In many cases, however, there is a partial solution to the dilemma. For many routines it is possible to formulate with a relatively small number of Boolean expressions what the routine will guarantee when it finishes executing.

Example In our abstract data type LIST in Chapter 3 we had the routines **add** and **remove** which added elements to the list or took them out again. The routine **add** guarantees that after execution of **add** (x) the Boolean expression

    has (x)

will yield **true**. And the routine **remove** guarantees that after execution of **remove** (x) the Boolean expression

    not has (x)

will yield **true**.

Such Boolean expressions that yield **true** upon termination of a routine will be called **postconditions**.

Now it is generally true that not every routine can, if it starts in an arbitrary starting state, do what it is supposed to do. It requires that the starting state fulfill certain conditions. In our function **gcd** for computing the greatest common divisor of two numbers m, n, we demanded that both m and n should be non-negative. Without this condition the correctness of the result cannot be guaranteed. Such conditions that must be fulfilled before a routine can begin its work will be called **preconditions**.

Bertrand Meyer, the author of the Eiffel language, speaks of a contract ('programming by contract') that each routine offers its potential callers: 'If you fulfill my preconditions then I guarantee to make my postconditions be true upon my return'. The preconditions describe the contractual duties of the caller, the postconditions those of the callee (routine).

The syntax of Eiffel routines now acquires new clauses with which the pre- and postconditions can be formulated. A procedure looks as follows:

```
proc_name (arg_list) is

    require
        -- the preconditons (Boolean expressions)

    local
        -- declarations of local entities

    do
        -- the body

    ensure
        -- the postconditions (Boolean expressions)
    end
```

and a function has the form

```
func_name (arg_list) : return_type is

    require
        -- the preconditions (Boolean expressions)

    local
        -- declarations of local entities

    do
        -- the body

    ensure
        -- the postconditions (Boolean expressions)
    end
```

These pre- and postconditions have a twofold role. On the one hand, they document for the reader of the class text what the routine needs in order to do its job and what it promises its callers. On the other hand, these conditions can (optionally) be checked by the running system while a program is being executed to make sure they are never violated. If they are violated the program will be terminated and a corresponding error message sent to the user.

Examples

1. We can now supply the routines add and remove from the class LIST with appropriate postconditions:

```
add (x : ELEMENT) is

    local
        n : NODE

    do
        if not has (x) then
            !!n
            n.set_item (x)
            n.set_next (first)
            first := n
            count := count + 1
        end

    ensure
        is_there : has (x)
    end
```

```
remove (x : ELEMENT) is

    local
        pre, post : NODE

    do
        from
            pre := first
        until
            pre = void or else equal (x, pre.item)
        loop
            post := pre
            pre  := pre.next
        end

        if pre /= void then        -- found!
            if post = void then    -- was 1st node
                first := pre.next
            else
                post.set_next (pre.next)
            end
```

```
                    count := count - 1
            end


        ensure
            is_gone : not has (x)
    end
```

Each of the Boolean expressions in a pre- or postcondition can be supplied optionally with a **label**. In add our label is is_there; and in remove it is is_gone. These labels are without semantic significance, but if a condition should be violated the label will be included in the error message sent to the user so that one can determine more readily which condition was violated. The reader is recommended always to provide pre- and postconditions with suitable labels.

2. In the function gcd in Chapter 2 we formulated the precondition as a comment because at that time we had nothing better. Now we can use a **require** clause:

```
    gcd (m, n : INTEGER) : INTEGER   is

        require
            non_negative : m >= 0 and then n >= 0

        do
            if n = 0 then
                result := m
            else
                result := gcd (n, m \\ n)
            end
    end
```

The pre- and postconditions are examples of the Eiffel **assertions**. They are not the only kinds of assertions that Eiffel has to offer. Another situation in which help in finding correct formulations is often needed is the loop construction. In proving that a complicated loop is correct it is often very helpful to find a **loop invariant**. This is a list of Boolean expressions that should evaluate to **true** on every pass through the loop. Ideally, the combination of the loop invariant with the termination condition (until clause) should produce exactly the statement that one wants to be true after execution of the loop. If one can then prove that the loop invariant is indeed preserved on each pass through the loop, then one has a complete proof of the correctness of the loop.

Another problem with loops is the demonstration that they terminate after finitely many iterations, i.e. that the termination test produces **true** after finitely many repetitions of the loop body. Loops not having this property are called **endless** loops and, of course, lead to programs that never terminate.

One possibility to guarantee the termination of a loop consists of finding an INTEGER expression that never becomes negative and that is decremented by at least one on each pass through the loop. If this expression has the value n after execution of the loop initialization, then obviously the loop must terminate after at most n iterations.

The syntax for loops in Eiffel has a corresponding extension as follows:

```
from
    -- the initialization

invariant
    -- the loop invariant

variant
    -- INTEGER expression that decreases on
    -- each pass but never becomes negative

until
    -- termination test

loop
    -- loop body

end
```

Example As an example of the use of Eiffel assertions we now present an algorithm for efficient searching for a particular element in a sorted list. With 'list' we really mean **Array**. An array is an abstract data type in which elements of an arbitrary type can be stored and later recovered. In this the arrays are very similar to our lists but every element in an array has a fixed position, an **index**, given by an integer. The element is stored at this position and can be recovered by giving the index. The most important operations are the following:

```
lower        -- lowest permissible index
upper        -- highest permissible index
count        -- identical with upper - lower + 1
put (x, n)   -- store element x at index n;
             -- overwrite previous value there
item (n)     -- return element at position n
make (m, n)  -- creation procedure; new array
             -- with lower = m, upper = n
```

This abstract data type is implemented in Eiffel by the standard class ARRAY.

We will now assume that the elements in the array are of a type that has a total order, i.e. a type possessing the operators <, >, <= and >= . The only such classes we've met so far are INTEGER and REAL. In Chapter 6 we will encounter others. Under the given assumption we may suppose that the elements in our array are *ordered* or *sorted*:

```
i < j implies a.item (i) <= a.item (j)
```

Using this assumption we can search for a given element in a very efficient manner using the method everyone uses when looking up a name in a telephone book or a word in a dictionary. One opens the book in the middle and compares a word found there with the one being sought. If the word being looked for precedes (lexicographically) the word in the dictionary, then we know our word must be in the first half of the book – if it is there at all. By repeatedly halving the set of pages still to be searched through using this method we very rapidly find the word we are looking up or else determine that it is not in the dictionary. One can easily convince oneself that at most k steps will be need if

$$2^k >= n$$

and n is the number of entries in the book. That is, with this method we need at most

$$\log_2(n)$$

steps.

Here, then, is the corresponding routine in Eiffel:

```
binary_search (a : ARRAY [ELEMENT], x : ELEMENT) is

    require
        non_trivial : a /= void and then a.count > 0
        is_sorted   : -- a is sorted in increasing order

    local
        low, mid, high : INTEGER

    do
        from
            low  := a.lower - 1
            high := a.upper + 1
        invariant
            a.lower - 1 <= low   and then
                   low < high  and then
                  high <= a.upper + 1
            low  = a.lower - 1 or else a.item (low) <= x
            high = a.upper + 1 or else x < a.item (high)
```

```
            variant
                high - low
            until
                low = high - 1
            loop
                mid := (low + high) // 2

                if a.item (mid) <= x then
                    low := mid
                else
                    high := mid
                end
            end

            check
                low >= a.lower - 1 and then low <= a.upper
                low  = a.lower - 1 or else a.item (low) <= x
                low  = a.upper or else x < a.item (low + 1)
            end

            found := (low >= a.lower and then x <= a.item (low))

            if found then
                index := low
            end

        ensure
            found : found implies (x <= a.item (index)
                                   and then
                                   x >= a.item (index))
    end
```

In this one example we have illustrated all the Eiffel assertions presented so far: pre- and postconditions as well as loop invariants and the **variant** clause. In addition we see here a further use of assertions: the **check** clause. A **check** clause may be used anywhere where an instruction would be legal. Between **check** and **end** we may have arbitrarily many Boolean expressions. When the flow of control during execution of the enclosing routine reaches the **check** clause all of these Boolean expressions will be evaluated (if assertion checking is turned on). They must all evaluate to **true**. If at least one of them does not, the program is terminated with an error message.

Our **check** clause above formulates just what we would like to be true after completion of the loop. The **check** clause is essentially the conjunction of the loop invariant with the termination test. It states that the element x being looked for is either at the position **low** or else it should be inserted between the elements at `low` and `low + 1`.

Remarks

1. The class `ARRAY` is in reality an example of a **generic** class, that is, a parameterized family of classes. The generic classes will not be treated until Chapter 8. Here it suffices to remark that an array can store elements of a quite arbitrary type. The type `T` of the elements to be stored is given between square brackets:

    ```
    a : ARRAY [T]
    ```

    In our example above we called the type `ELEMENT`.
2. The entities `found` and `index` were not declared in our example. We have assumed that they are attributes of the enclosing class.
3. One is tempted to make our routine `binary_search` into a function of type `BOOLEAN`. The result would be `true` precisely when the element being sought were actually found. Then we could do without the attribute `found`. But then our function would have side effects: the attribute `index` is modified. We resolved in the preceding chapter not to write functions with side effects.
4. It is comparatively easy to check the correctness of our routine `binary_search`. First one shows that the loop invariant is indeed true right after the loop initialization and after every repetition of the loop body. Then one demonstrates that the assertions in the `check` clause follow logically from the conjunction of the loop invariant with the termination test. The assertion in the `ensure` clause follows immediately from the `check` clause together with the `if found then` instruction. The postcondition formulates the condition in which one is mainly interested when calling `binary_search`.

One can often formulate the properties or axioms that must hold using the Eiffel language, i.e. with `BOOLEAN` expressions, as we did in the example above. Sometimes, however, the condition is too complex to be formulated as an Eiffel expression. In such cases one should nevertheless include the corresponding assertion and replace the `BOOLEAN` expression by an appropriate comment formulating the property in natural language. The runtime system cannot of course test such assertions but the important function of documenting the code is still achieved.

Example

```
from
    m := left
    i := m + 1
```

```
invariant
    m < i
    -- a[left + 1 .. m] < pivot
    -- pivot <= a[m + 1 .. i - 1]
variant
    right - i + 1
until
    i = right + 1
loop
    ...
```

In this piece of code, taken from the sorting routine `quicksort` (cf. [Ref. 3] p. 112), we were not able to formulate the invariant as a BOOLEAN expression in Eiffel. But it is important here to know what the invariant is, so we write it in an intuitive notation meaning 'all array elements from `left + 1` to `m` are smaller than `pivot` and all array elements from `m + 1` to `i - 1` are greater than or equal to `pivot`'.

One reason why one has to resort to comments in assertions is that we have no logical quantifiers 'for all' and 'there exist' in Eiffel.

The programmer is urged to look carefully for loop invariants of any non-trivial loop and to formulate them as `invariant` clauses when he finds them. If a loop does not seem to have a sensible invariant, this could be a clue that the loop is not well formulated.

One important Eiffel assertion has not yet been mentioned: the class invariant. The Boolean expressions in the class invariant define conditions that must be true of *all* objects of the class at all *stable* times. 'Stable time' essentially means upon exit from a routine of the class. During the execution of a routine the class invariant may be temporarily violated. Thus all routines of the class must guarantee that upon their completion not only their postconditions but also the class invariants are satisfied. On the other hand, every routine can assume that when it begins executing, not only its preconditions but also the class invariants are satisfied.

The syntax of the class text is expanded correspondingly by a further clause:

```
class CLASS_NAME

creation
    -- list of creation procedures
feature
    -- list of attributes and routines
invariant
    -- the class invariants

end -- class CLASS_NAME
```

We can illustrate this idea with a simple example. We give an implementation for the complex numbers that supports their being represented either in cartesian or in polar coordinates:

```
class COMPLEX

creation
    make_rect, make_polar

feature


    x     : REAL -- real part
    y     : REAL -- imaginary part
    rho   : REAL -- absolute value
    theta : REAL -- angle to the x-axis


    epsilon : REAL is 1.0E-6


-----------------------------------------------------------------


    make_rect (r, i : REAL) is

        do
            x     := r
            y     := i
            rho   := sqrt (x ^ 2 + y ^ 2)
            theta := arctan2 (y, x)
        end
-----------------------------------------------------------------


    make_polar (r, t : REAL) is

        do
            rho   := r
            theta := t
            x     := rho * cos (theta)
            y     := rho * sin (theta)
        end
-----------------------------------------------------------------
```

```
    infix "+" (other : COMPLEX) : COMPLEX is

        do
            !!result.make_rect (x + other.x, y + other.y)
        end
```

```
    infix "*" (other : COMPLEX) : COMPLEX is

        do
            !!result.make_polar (rho * other.rho,
                                 theta + other.theta)
        end
```

```
    ...


invariant
    consistent : abs (x, rho * cos (theta)) < epsilon
                 and then
                 abs (y, rho * sin (theta)) < epsilon

end -- class COMPLEX
```

Remarks

1. The class invariant formulates the condition that the two representations of a complex number are consistent with one another, i.e. they differ by at most a small amount `epsilon`.
2. The reader may well wonder where the functions `arctan2`, `sin`, `cos`, `sqrt` and **abs** come from. We cannot answer this question until the next chapter.
3. The implementation given here is suitable for illustrating the use of class invariants. It is, however, somewhat unrealistic. In practice, one would almost certainly prefer to implement one of the representations – say the cartesian – with attributes and the other with functions. That could look as follows:

```
class COMPLEX

creation
    make_rect, make_polar

feature

    x : REAL -- real part
```

```
    y : REAL -- imaginary part


    ------------------------------------------------------------


    make_rect (r, i : REAL) is

        do
            x := r
            y := i
        end
    ------------------------------------------------------------


    make_polar (r, t : REAL) is

        do
            x := r * cos (t)
            y := r * sin (t)
        end
    ------------------------------------------------------------


    rho : REAL is

        do
            result := sqrt (x ^ 2 + y ^ 2)
        end
    ------------------------------------------------------------


    theta : REAL is

        do
            result := arctan2 (y, x)
        end
    ------------------------------------------------------------



        . . .


end -- class COMPLEX
```

A user of this class would not be able to distinguish it from the one given previously. But every object of type **COMPLEX** would now only have two attributes of type **REAL** instead of four and would thus occupy less space in main memory. The routines **make_rect** and **make_polar** would also be faster.

The creation procedures are an exception to the rule that every routine may assume the class invariant when it is called. When an object is created, all its entities are initialized with the default values. It can happen that these default values do not satisfy the class invariant. It is the job of the creation procedures to guarantee that the invariants are satisfied. This is the reason that the syntax combines the calling of a creation procedure with the creation instruction; after both have been carried out the class invariant is fulfilled. However, one cannot then demand that the invariant be true upon entering a creation procedure; it is the task of the creation procedure to make the invariant true.

We should mention at this point that external routines can also be provided with pre- and postconditions. The extended form for external procedures, for example, is then as follows:

```
pname (arg1 : T1; arg2 : T2; ...; argn : Tn) is

    require
        -- here the preconditions

    external "C"
    alias "other_name"

    ensure
        -- here the postconditions
    end
```

The preconditions are checked before the external routine is called and the post-conditions are checked after the external routine returns. In this way the use of external routines can be made almost as secure as that of internal routines.

5.2 Exceptions

Up to now we have talked as if the violation of an assertion always leads to the termination of the program. The truth is more complicated but also provides for a flexible reaction to any kind of error.

In Eiffel the idea of a contract between a routine and its caller is taken very seriously. Every effort is made to prevent a routine from being dishonest, i.e. pretending to have fulfilled its contract when in fact it has not. This means that an Eiffel routine can only return to its caller in one of two states:

- Success: the routine has completely fulfilled its contract.
- Error: the routine could not fulfill its contract (for whatever reason) and admits it.

In the second case the Eiffel runtime system 'raises' an **exception**. This means that the calling procedure is also confronted with an error condition. If it does not attempt to deal with the error (we shall soon see how to do that), then it, too, ends in the state 'error'. In this way the error propagates upwards through the chain of routine calls until either some routine fixes the error or the creation procedure of the root object is reached. Here the chain ends and at this point the program is aborted.

But there is another possibility, as we have already indicated. A routine in the call chain can attempt to repair the error. In programs that are used only by their author, reacting to errors by aborting may be acceptable. In programs that are used by many people, an 'error tolerant' behavior is expected. Users are almost never satisfied with a program that prints an error message on the screen and gives up.

A routine that wants to pull the bacon out of the fire needs a `rescue` clause, a language element that we have not yet seen. A procedure, for example, with a `rescue` clause looks as follows:

```
proc_name (arg_list) is

    require
        -- the preconditions (Boolean expressions)

    local
        -- declarations of local entities

    do
        -- the body

    ensure
        -- the postconditions (Boolean expressions)

    rescue
        -- error handling

    end
```

The instructions in the `rescue` clause are only executed if an exception occurs in the body of the routine. In particular, they are not executed if a precondition is violated, because in that case the body is never reached. The most important task of the `rescue` clause is to return the current object to a consistent state by ensuring that the class invariants are satisfied.

If the end of the `rescue` clause is reached, then the enclosing routine still ends in the state 'error', i.e. the exception is not cancelled. The error tolerant aspect comes in by way of an instruction that we have not previously seen since it may only occur in a `rescue` clause: the `retry` instruction. A `retry` instruction causes two things to happen:

- The exception is cancelled.
- The body of the routine is executed once more beginning at the top.

Using a `retry` instruction only makes sense, of course, if one has a reasonable hope that a new try could succeed. The following example illustrates a possible use of the `retry` clause:

```
clever_proc is

    local
        tries : INTEGER

    do
        if tries = 0 then
            -- the first strategy
        else
            -- an alternative strategy
        end

    rescue
        tries := tries + 1

        if tries < 2 then
            retry
        end
    end
```

When our procedure `clever_proc` is called the local entity `tries` is initialized with the default value 0. Thus on the first pass through the routine body the first strategy is selected. If the first strategy does not lead to an exception then the routine ends in the state 'success'. If, however, the first strategy causes an error, control is transferred to the `rescue` clause. There, `tries` is assigned the value 1 and the body is tried again. This time the alternative strategy is chosen. If the alternative succeeds, then the routine itself succeeds. But if the alternative also causes an exception, then the `rescue` clause is once again executed and `tries` is now set to 2. This time the end of the `rescue` clause is reached and the whole routine ends in failure.

Let us examine the reasons that can lead to the failure of a routine. We shall also want to know in each case 'Who is to blame?'.

- A precondition is violated. In this case the calling routine is at fault.
- Some other assertion in the routine is violated: an **invariant**, **variant**, **check** or **ensure** clause. In this case our routine is to blame and must be repaired.
- A routine that is called in the body of our routine returns in the state 'error'. If it failed because its precondition was violated, then, again, our routine is to blame. Otherwise the problem lies in a 'deeper' layer – possibly at the bottom, i.e. in the physical machine. Perhaps a hard disk is full or the network connection has gone down.

The Eiffel assertions consist of one or several Boolean expressions and these in turn can involve calling functions. Thus it is a priori conceivable that an error could occur during the execution of one of these functions. In that case our list above would be incomplete. In reality, however, the exception raising mechanism is turned off while assertions are being checked in order to avoid such 'cascading' error situations. But if one writes assertions that contain erroneous function calls, then some very inscrutable error situations can occur.

We conclude this chapter with the remark that it can *never* be the task of a **rescue** clause to fulfill the contract of the enclosing routine. That is the exclusive duty and prerogative of the routine body. The **rescue** clause has the job of bringing the current object back into a consistent state. In cases where it appears appropriate, the **rescue** clause can use the **retry** instruction to give the routine body a new chance. In any case control must return to the routine body if the routine is to end in the state 'success', because if the end of the **rescue** clause is reached, then the end state is automatically 'error'.

5.3   Exercises

1. In your iterative solution for Ex. 1, Chapter 3 you presumably used a loop. Provide that loop with appropriate **invariant** and **variant** clauses. Your loop invariant should have the property that its conjunction with the termination condition gives exactly what the routine **power** is supposed to guarantee. Prove that your invariant is indeed preserved by each pass through the body of the loop.

2. Program your favorite sorting algorithm in Eiffel and supply the loop (or loops) with appropriate **invariant** clauses. If possible, the invariants should be Boolean expressions; if not, then suitable comments. In any case you should make sure that your 'invariants' genuinely are invariant and that their conjunction with the termination test does indeed imply the assertion that the array is sorted.

Chapter 6

Inheritance

6.1 Specialization and generalization

A programming language that deserves the appellation 'object-oriented' must have at least two properties:

- Every data object must be an instance of a class. This idea was discussed in Chapter 4.
- The language must support the mechanism of **inheritance** between classes. This chapter's task is to introduce the inheritance mechanism as it is implemented in Eiffel.

Not only do we categorize the objects of the real world and our mental world into classes; we also employ relationships between these classes. One of the most fundamental of these relationships is that of **specialization**. A class B is a specialization of a class A if every instance of B has all the properties and all the behavior of objects from class A. In general, the instances of B will also have additional properties and additional behavior that instances of A need not have – in particular those properties and that behavior that characterize objects of type B. Thus the class of vicious dogs is a specialization of the class of all dogs; and the class of dogs is a specialization of the class of mammals. Or the class of procedural languages is a specialization of the class of all programming languages; and programming languages in turn are a specialization of the class of formal languages.

When we are explaining to a listener what a vicious dog is, it is a great help if we may assume that the listener knows what a dog is. Then we can simply say that a vicious dog is a dog that bites innocent postmen – or something of the sort. Most of the properties of a vicious dog are in fact those that the animal has in its quality of being a dog; but we save ourselves the trouble of enumerating all these many properties by taking these properties as known.

Now there are situations in real life and in the sciences where our classification schemes form a hierarchy – or tree, as a computer scientist would say. Each class is a specialization of at most one other class – it's **parent class** (or superclass, as it is called in some object-oriented languages). An example of such a hierarchical classification is the Linnean classification of all living organisms.

Such hierarchical or tree-like classification schemes are, however, the exception rather than the rule. Usually, a class is more naturally regarded as a specialization of several other classes. Thus the class of cities can be regarded as a specialization of geographical locations. But cities can also be regarded as a particular kind of social organization, or as a special kind of political structure.

Many object-oriented languages only support hierarchical classification or so-called **simple inheritance**. This is partly in order to simplify the implementation. But it can also be regarded as a simplification for the programmer, who may find it easier to think about tree-like structures, where each class has at most one parent or superclass. Other languages take the point of view that allowing a class to be a specialization of several other classes permits a more realistic modelling of the world that one is trying to model with a computer program. These languages are said to support **multiple inheritance**. Eiffel belongs to the latter category.

Inheritance (whether simple or multiple) is a significant aid to the constructor of software for at least three reasons:

- Inheritance often permits a more realisitic model of a part of the world, as we just remarked. Thus we might have a class SHIP and, as specializations of this class, further classes SAILING_SHIP, FREIGHT_SHIP, PASSENGER_SHIP, FISHING_TRAWLER, WAR_SHIP. Each of these classes could be further specialized as needed, say KETCH, YAWL, CATAMARAN, etc., as specializations of SAILING_SHIP.
- When defining a class B that is a specialization of another class A we need only specify those features of B that are not found in A. Often, these are only a few features. In a programming language without inheritance we would be forced to use the cut and paste features of the editor to copy all the features of A into B. This makes it more difficult to understand and to maintain the class texts. Every change in A requires a corresponding change in B.
- Inheritance makes **polymorphism** possible. This term means that an entity x of type T may be bound to objects of differing types at different times as long as they all understand all the 'messages' that objects of type T are expected to understand.

The concept of polymorphism is not likely to be familiar to many readers. Therefore, we pause to give an example of its use before we begin to show its use in general.

Example In a model of a company we could have a class PERSON that models the properties that people have in general. As a specialization of this class we might have classes CUSTOMER and EMPLOYEE, each of which has the more specific

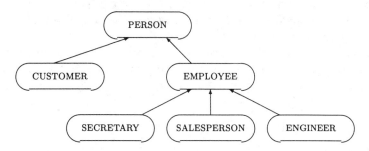

Figure 6.1 An inheritance graph

properties typical of these two groups of people, say `acct_nr` for `CUSTOMER` and `salary` for `EMPLOYEE`. The class `EMPLOYEE` is then further specialized to reflect the various kinds of employees in the company, say `SECRETARY`, `SALESPERSON`, `ENGINEER`. The corresponding inheritanace diagram is shown in Fig. 6.1.

Now, for each kind of employee the way in which the monthly paycheck is computed is typical for this class. So each of the employee classes will need a suitable routine `months_pay`. In a language without inheritance it would be necessary to give each of these `months_pay` routines a unique name, say `secretary_pay`, `salesperson_pay`, `engineer_pay`, since it is usually not permissible to use the same name for different routines.

In a language with inheritance the compiler and the runtime system make sure that in every case the correct `months_pay` routine is called. Then we could have a collection of employees, of which some are secretaries, some are salespeople and some are engineers. We could iterate through the collection and call the `months_pay` routine for each employee without worrying about what kind of job he or she has. The system makes sure that the correct version of `months_pay` is called in each case.

In a language without inheritance the body of this loop might look as follows (using Eiffel syntax):

```
inspect emp.type
when Secretary_type then
    pay := secretary_pay (emp)
when Salesperson_type then
    pay := salesperson_pay (emp)
when Engineer_type then
    pay := engineer_pay (emp)
end
```

In Eiffel, on the other hand, the block of code above can be replaced by the one line

```
pay := emp.months_pay
```

The runtime system makes sure that the correct `months_pay` routine is called.

In Chapter 3 we remarked that the multibranch instruction is seldom used in Eiffel. Now we see the reason for that remark.

One should point out here that if at some later time a further class of employee is introduced, say `JANITOR`, the multibranch above must be extended with a further case:

```
when Janitor_type then
      pay := janitor_pay (emp)
```

In Eiffel (and other languages supporting inheritance) absolutely no change to the loop would be necessary – no matter how many employee classes might be introduced after the fact.

Up to now we have talked as if a child class follows its parent chronologically. This is true if the operation used is specialization. But the opposite of specialization is *generalization* and this can often be a useful operation when designing software. We discover that a number of classes that we have already designed have a significant number of properties, or much behavior, in common. Then it can be sensible to define a more general class from which the already existing classes can inherit. The common properties and common behavior are then moved up to the new parent. One also calls this 'factoring'.

We can illustrate this process of generalization using our example with the workers in a company. Let us suppose that we had the task of designing a model for the personnel structure of a company. We would begin by looking for suitable classes of objects for the model. It is likely that we would very quickly hit upon the classes `SECRETARY`, `SALESPERSON`, `DEPARTMENT_HEAD`, etc. After developing a number of such classes we notice that they all seem to have several attributes and several routines in common such as `name` or `months_pay`. After thinking the matter over we come to the conclusion that all of these classes have a common generalization: `EMPLOYEE`. So we create this new class and push the common attributes and routines up into this new class and let the others inherit from `EMPLOYEE`.

This process of generalization, or factorization, has several advantages. One is that the structure of our model becomes clearer: common properties of several classes become visible in the class structure. Another is that the classes `SECRETARY`, etc., become smaller and simpler; the common features have moved up to a more abstract class. The features that remain are those that are characteristic for these more specialized classes. A third advantage is that polymorphism now becomes possible, as we saw above. This allows such uniform solutions as the one we gave for computing the paycheck.

Now it could happen that at some later time we are asked to expand our model to include further aspects of the company, for example sales. In carrying out this extension we introduce the class `CUSTOMER` and discover that it has several things in common with `EMPLOYEE`, e.g. the attribute `name`. Therefore, we decide to introduce a further generalization: the class `PERSON` is produced and both `CUSTOMER` and `EMPOLYEE` now inherit from `PERSON`. One interesting aspect of this step is that users of the existing class EMPLOYEE (the clients) will not be affected by this change. The class text of EMPLOYEE will become smaller, since several features were factored into PERSON. But the set of features of EMPLOYEE remains the same and so does the externally visible behavior of this class.

The processes of specialization and generalization play an extremely important role in the design of models and systems in software development.

It is time to see how inheritance is expressed in Eiffel, where the specialized class is said to be a **child** class. Thus if B is a specialization of A, we say that B is a child of A or inherits from A. One also says that A is a **parent** of B. This is expressed by using an inherit clause in the class text of B. The class text is now as follows:

```
class CNAME

inherit
      -- here list of classes
      -- from which CNAME inherits

creation
      -- here the name(s) of
      -- creation procedure(s)

feature
        -- here the declarations and
        -- definitions of all features

invariant
        -- here the class invariants

end -- class CNAME
```

We said that Eiffel supports multiple inheritance. This is reflected in the fact that the inherit clause may contain arbitrarily many names of other classes.

As we said earlier, inheritance means that the new class automatically acquires *all* features of the classes from which it inherits – attributes as well as routines. Thus the **feature** clause of the new class need only contain the declarations and definitions of those features which are new in this class.

The same is true of the invariant clause. All invariants of the parent classes are automatically taken over by the child class. If the new class has an invariant clause, then the new invariants are in addition to those that are inherited. The effect is precisely that of taking the logical **and** of all the invariants from all parents plus the new invariants.

There is a sound ideological reason for the inheritance of class invariants. If class B is a child of class A (i.e. inherits from A), then every instance of B *is*, among other things, an A. Thus it must guarantee everything that an A guarantees, and possibly more as well.

Example Suppose the class GRAPH represents undirected graphs and we derive
a class FOREST from GRAPH with a class invariant `acyclic` (forests are undirected
graphs without cycles). Then we might derive a third class TREE from FOREST
with the additional invariant `connected`. Then every instance of TREE must not
only take care to preserve the invariant `connected`; it must also guarantee the
truth of `acyclic`.

The `creation` clause, on the other hand, is *not* inherited. If the child class is
to have creation routines, then they must be explicitly declared with a `creation`
clause – even if the creation procedures are in fact the same as in the parent
class.

Let us look at our example with persons and customers again:

```
class PERSON

inherit
    SYSTEM_TIME;
    MATH

creation
    make

feature

    name      : STRING
    address   : STRING
    telephone : STRING
    birthday  : REAL


--------------------------------------------------------------


    make (n : STRING, bd : REAL) is

        do
            name     := n
            birthday := bd
        end
--------------------------------------------------------------


    age : INTEGER is

        do
            result := floor ((now - birthday) / 365.0)
        end
--------------------------------------------------------------
```

```
    set_address (ad : STRING) is

        do
            address := ad
        end
--------------------------------------------------------------


    set_telephone (tn : STRING) is

        do
            telephone := tn
        end
--------------------------------------------------------------


    ...


class -- PERSON
```

Remarks

- Here we see a use of inheritance that is very common in Eiffel, although it does not fit in with our concept that inheritance expresses specialization; it is often used to acquire needed constants, attributes and routines from other classes. In this example it is the attribute `now` from the class `SYSTEM_TIME` and the function `floor` from the class `MATH`. In the preceding chapter we left the question unanswered where the class `COMPLEX` acquires the mathematical functions `sin`, `cos`, `arctan2`. Now we see that `COMPLEX` merely needs to inherit from `MATH`.

    This use of the inheritance mechanism is theoretically unsatisfying, for, after all, the concept 'person' is in no way a specialization of the concept 'system time'. From a theoretical standpoint it would be better if Eiffel provided some other mechanism for allowing a new class to acquire features from another class without implying that the new class is a specialization of the old one.

- The class `SYSTEM_TIME` is a class provided with the standard library of Eiffel/S. It is not a part of the language definition and will probably not be available in other implementations of Eiffel.

    In `SYSTEM_TIME`, time is treated as a real number. The unit of time is one day and the value of the attribute `now` is current Greenwich Mean Time. Thus we can compute the age of a person by subtracting his or her birthday from `now` and dividing by 365 (provided the time recorded in `birthday` is also in Greenwich Mean Time). This method is, however, not quite accurate, since it takes no account of leap years. We leave it as an exercise for the reader to investigate the class `SYSTEM_TIME` and find a way to compute `age` precisely.

- The function `floor` from the class `MATH` takes a real number as argument and returns the largest integer that is less than or equal to the argument.
- Why did we implement `age` as a function rather than as an attribute? Because a person's age changes continually whereas a birthdate is constant. If we had implemented the function `age` in a precise fashion, then it would have returned a correct result no matter when it was called.

We can now show the class CUSTOMER:

```
class CUSTOMER

inherit
    PERSON

creation
    make

feature

    balance : REAL

-------------------------------------------------------------

    pay_in (amount : REAL) is

        do
            balance := balance + amount
        end
-------------------------------------------------------------

    charge (amount : REAL) is

        require
            solvent : amount <= balance

        do
            balance := balance - amount
        end

end -- class CUSTOMER
```

Remarks

- In this case we have used inheritance in the way it was originally intended to be used: a 'customer' is indeed a specialization of the concept 'person'.

- We do not need to repeat the attributes and routines from the class PERSON like `name` or `set_address`. They will be inherited.
- On the other hand, the creation clause does need to be repeated. This clause is not automatically inherited from PERSON, although of course the routine `make` is.
- Here we made the design decision that customers are not allowed to overdraw their accounts. Therefore, we include the precondition

```
require
      solvent : amount <= balance
```

If we had wanted to allow overdrawn accounts, then of course we would leave out this precondition.

We have by no means described the full form of the `inherit` clause. It can in fact be rather complex. A first approximation is the following:

```
inherit
      C1
            rename
                  f1 as g1,
                  f2 as g2,
                  ...
            redefine
                  h1, h2, ...
            end;
      C2
            rename
                  ...
            redefine
                  ...
            end;
      ...
```

That is, in taking over features from class C1, one has the choice of renaming some of them and redefining some others (one may not do both at once for the same feature in the same parent clause).

Remark Here we see the second of the two constructs where the language definition makes a semicolon obligatory. Lists of parent classes are to be separated by semicolons. There should be no semicolon after the last parent in the list.

6.2 Redefining features

Let us look at redefinition first. We have already seen a case where redefinition of a feature is useful: the monthly pay routine for employees. For each special kind of employee we shall need a different procedure `months_pay`. Thus in each of the classes that inherit from `EMPLOYEE` we will redefine the feature `months_pay`.

```
class SECRETARY

inherit
    EMPLOYEE
        redefine
            months_pay
        end

creation
    make

feature
    hours_worked : REAL -- hours in this month
    hourly_wage  : REAL
-----------------------------------------------------------------

    months_pay : REAL is

        do
            result := hourly_wage * hours_worked
        end
-----------------------------------------------------------------

    set_hours (hrs : REAL) is

        do
            hours_worked := hrs
        end

end -- class SECRETARY
```

The salesperson is paid according to a different system. He or she receives a fixed monthly salary but in addition there is a bonus based on the number of sales made.

```
class SALESPERSON

inherit
    EMPLOYEE
        redefine
            months_pay
        end
```

```
creation
    make

feature

    salary : REAL
    bonus  : REAL

-------------------------------------------------------------

    months_pay : REAL is

        do
            result := salary + bonus
        end
-------------------------------------------------------------

    set_bonus (b : REAL) is

        do
            bonus := b
        end

end -- class SALESPERSON
```

For engineers the matter is extremely simple: an engineer gets a fixed salary and nothing more. Not even overtime is taken into consideration. In this case it is sensible to redefine `months_pay` as an attribute. That is permissible in Eiffel, although the reverse direction is forbidden: redefining an attribute as function. (The reader should think about why this kind of redefinition cannot be allowed.)

```
class ENGINEER

inherit
    EMPLOYEE
        redefine
            months_pay
        end

creation
    make

feature
```

```
    months_pay : REAL


  ------------------------------------------------------------

    set_salary (s : REAL) is

      do
          months_pay := s
      end

end -- class ENGINEER
```

Remark The routine `months_pay` that is being redefined here is inherited from
the parent class **EMPLOYEE**. The reader may well have wondered how the corresponding routine in that class might look. The question is justified; the class
EMPLOYEE is so general or abstract that one cannot give a prescription for computing the monthly pay there. This question will be answered in Section 6.7.

Now the routines are intended to express the characteristic behavior of a class.
Thus the point of redefining a routine should of course be to make the behavior
more specific – not to alter it into some quite different behavior. Thus it would
be perverse to redefine the `months_pay` routine in **SECRETARY** so that it computed
the number of days since Christmas. There is no way in which the compiler can
prevent the programmer from committing such perversities in general. However,
we do have the assertions and, in particular, the postconditions of routines,
which are supposed to formulate what the routine guarantees to provide. Thus
one would expect that the postconditions of the redefined routine should be at
least as strong as those of the original routine.

For this reason the postconditions of the original routine are automatically inherited by the redefined routine, which can, at most, strengthen them by adding
still further postconditions. This is emphasized by the syntax. New postconditions are added in the redefined routine by the clause

```
  ensure then
        new postconditions
```

Just as with the class invariants of the child class the Eiffel compiler forms
the logical **and** of the new postconditions with those inherited from the original
routine.

What about the preconditions? Should they also be strenghtened – or instead
weakened?

In accordance with the Eiffel philosophy of 'programming by contract' the
preconditions may only be weakened. This amounts to saying: the redefined
routine must be prepared to take on any job that the original routine would
have accepted. Thus it may not tighten the acceptance conditions. The Eiffel
compiler achieves this by forming the logical **or** of the new preconditions with

those inherited from the original routine. The syntax emphasizes this fact with the formulation

```
require else
    new preconditions
```

which must be used in redefined routines.

What about the formal arguments of the redefined routine? Must they have the same number and types as those of the original routine? As far as the number is concerned, the answer is 'Yes'. The answer about the types is: 'The new types must conform to the old types'. Since we cannot as yet define what conformance means, we postpone the discussion of this matter for a little. Suffice it to say that it is in any case correct to leave the types of the arguments unchanged.

The same is true of the types of attributes and functions. Thus, for the moment, it appears that it would be pointless to redefine an attribute. However, we shall see that it can be quite useful to redefine an attribute to be of a new (conforming) type.

Eiffel provides a means to prevent redefinition of a feature when the author of a class believes that redefining the feature would be harmful or senseless. These are the **frozen** features:

```
frozen fname (...) : T is ...
```

defines a function **fname** that may not be redefined in any descendent; it is frozen. One should only make use of this possibility when it really seems unavoidable. In many cases where one may decide to make a feature frozen it is a good idea to provide a non-frozen version of the same feature. To this end one can use the so-called *synonyms*.

Example

```
equal, frozen standard_equal (other : like current) : BOOLEAN is
    ...
```

is an example from the class **GENERAL**. Here two different versions of **equal** are defined, one frozen, the other not frozen. In most cases they are identical. However, in situations where one may need another version of **equal**, one may redefine it. The standard version is then still available as **standard_equal** and is guaranteed to be the original version since it can never be redefined.

6.3 Renaming features

There are at least two reasons why one might wish to rename an inherited feature:

* to have a name more suitable to the new class,

- to avoid name clashes when inheriting from several classes having features
  with the same name.

We can illustrate the first use of renaming with the following example.

Example   Suppose we have a class GRAPH describing general purpose graphs and
we want to specialize to a new class INHERIT_GRAPH of graphs describing the
inheritance relation between classes in an object-oriented language. Then part
of the inherit clause might look something like the following:

```
inherit
    GRAPH
        rename
            add_vertex as add_class,
            add_edge   as add_relation,
            ...
```

That is, we are using renaming to give some features names that are more appropriate in the new context.

The second use of renaming is dictated by the necessity of having a unique
name for each feature of a class. It is not forbidden for two different classes to
have a feature with the same name – say f. These two features need not have
anything to do with each other. If, now, a third class should inherit from both
these classes, it would have two distinct features, both with the name f. This is
what we call a **name clash**. Something must be done.

One could in principle demand that one of the two parent classes be changed;
the feature f in one of them would be renamed as, say, f1. Then the name clash
disappears. A moment's reflection shows, however, that this is a poor solution.
The two classes from which one wishes to inherit could very well be two old, well
established classes that have been used in many software projects. Altering one
of them now would mean having to alter all the software in which they have been
employed. This is clearly an unsatisfactory way of dealing with the problem.

The solution chosen by Eiffel is to allow the child class to refer to one (or even
both) of the two conflicting features by a different name. Then it is clear in the
context of the new class which feature is meant.

Example   Suppose we have classes A and B and both have a feature f. Suppose
we want to derive a new class C that is to inherit from A and B. We resolve the
name clash as follows:

```
class C

inherit
    A
        rename f as g
        end;
```

```
      B

feature

   ...


    h(x, y : T) is

       do
           g (x, y)    -- this is the routine
                       -- known as f in class A
           f (y)       -- this routine is
                       -- inherited from B

           ...
       end

end -- class C
```

6.4 Export policy

We saw in Chapter 4 that one could control the export of features by using multiple **feature** clauses in a class. Each **feature** clause stipulates to which classes its features are to be exported.

A child class may wish to depart from the export policy laid down by its parents. This, too, can be achieved in the **inherit** clause. Between the **rename** and the **redefine** clauses one may have an **export** clause such as the following:

```
inherit
     C
        rename
           ...
        export
            { D, E, F, ...}
                f, g, h, ...
            { M, N, ... }
                k, l, m
        redefine
           ...
        end
```

Here the child class is laying down a new export policy: the features f, g, h, ... are now to be exported to the classes D, E, F, ... regardless of their export status in the parent C. Similarly, the features k, l, m, ... are now to be exported to the classes M, N, ...

6.5   An example

There are many situations in which multiple inheritance seems quite natural and useful. Let us look at an example.

Example   Modern graphical user interfaces (GUIs) employ **windows** to manage the information presented on the screen. Windows have, among others, the following properties and behavior:

- A window is a rectangular region on the screen defined by a width and a height (in pixels) and by the pixel coordinates of the upper left corner. In addition, the window might involve a mapping (or transformation) from world coordinates (application coordinates) to pixel coordinates.
- A window can have subwindows – often called its children. The subwindows in turn also have subwindows. Thus the windows form a tree.

These two aspects of a window are actually independent of one another (one often says *orthogonal* to one another). This is a typical situation for multiple inheritance. We might, therefore, be well advised to let the new class `WINDOW` that we are designing inherit from classes `TREE` and `CANVAS`, where the class `CANVAS` describes a rectangular area on which one can draw.

The class `TREE` might look as follows:

```
class TREE

creation
    make

feature

    parent   : TREE
    children : COLLECTION [like parent]
--------------------------------------------------------

    make is

        do
            !!children
        end
--------------------------------------------------------

    set_parent (p : like parent) is

        do
            parent := p
        end
```

```
--------------------------------------------------------

    add_child (c : like parent) is

        do
            children.add (c)
        end
--------------------------------------------------------


    . . .


end -- class TREE
```

Here, for the first time, we see an example of **anchored declaration** or **anchored types** using the reserved word like. It will become clear in a moment why this is useful. At any rate, it should be clear what it means: the entity children is a COLLECTION of things of the same type as parent, i.e. of type TREE (COLLECTION is a generic class, that is, a parameterized family of classes. These will be treated in Chapter 8). And the arguments of set_parent and add_child are both of the same type as parent – again TREE.

We shall not describe the class CANVAS more explicitly. It will, of course, have attributes width, height, etc.

Now, however, we can describe the class WINDOW:

```
class WINDOW

inherit
    TREE
        rename
            make        as tree_make,
            add_child as add_subwindow
        redefine
            parent
        end;

    CANVAS
        rename
            make as canvas_make
        end

creation
    make

feature

    parent : WINDOW
```

```
------------------------------------------------------------

    make is

        do
            tree_make
            canvas_make
        end
------------------------------------------------------------

        -- possibly further features not inherited

end -- class WINDOW
```

Now we can understand how useful anchored declaration using `like` is. By merely redefining the one attribute `parent` as being of type `WINDOW` we have also achieved the following:

- The attribute `children` of the class `WINDOW` is now a collection of `WINDOW`, not just `TREE`.
- The arguments of `set_parent` and `add_child` (renamed `add_subwindow`) are now of type `WINDOW`.

An anchored declaration

```
    x : like y
```

is valid if `y` is an attribute or a formal argument that is not itself of an anchored type. In particular, `y` may be the special entity `current`. In Section 6.7 we shall see examples where `like current` is frequently used.

6.6   Conformance

We are now in a position to define when a type `B` **conforms to** a type `A`. Remember that the concepts of *type* and *class* are actually equivalent. We shall also need the concepts of ancestor and descendent. A class `A` is an **ancestor** of a class `B` if

- `A` and `B` are the same class or
- recursively `A` is an ancestor of a parent of `B`.

`A` is called a **proper** ancestor of `B` if `A` is an ancestor of `B` and they are not the same class.

A class `B` is a **descendent** of a class `A` if `A` is an ancestor of `B`. And `B` is a **proper** descendent of `A` if `B` is a descendent of `A` and they are not the same class.

Definition
Let the type S be given by the class A and the type T by the class B. Then T **conforms to** S if and only if B is a descendent of A.

This is actually only a preliminary definition. When we come to the generic classes in Chapter 8 we will have to revise the definition of conformance slightly.

It is clear that conformance is a transitive relation. That is, if T conforms to S and U conforms to T, then U conforms to S.

Examples A WINDOW thus conforms to a TREE and also to a CANVAS. A SAILING_SHIP conforms to a SHIP and so does a CATAMARAN.

Conformance plays a role in the following situations:

- An assignment

    x := y

  is only allowed if the type of the expression y conforms to the type of entity x. This means, in particular, that any object to which y might be bound will have a type conforming to the type of y and thus also to the type of x (transitivity).
- The actual arguments in a routine call must have types conforming to the types of the corresponding formal arguments.

  This rule is really just a special case of the previous rule. For during a routine call the values of the actual arguments are bound to the formal arguments.
- When redefining an attribute we are only allowed to replace the type of the attribute with a new type conforming to the old type. This is precisely what we did with the attribute **parent** in the class WINDOW above.
- When redefining a function we are only allowed to replace the return type of the function by a new type conforming to the old type.

  Since the return type of a function is in effect a special postcondition ('I guarantee that the object returned will be a descendent of T'), this is essentially a strengthening of the postconditions – just what we demand when redefining.
- When redefining a routine we are not permitted to change the number of formal arguments. But we are allowed to replace the type of each argument by a conforming type.

  Note that the types of the formal arguments are a kind of precondition: 'I require that the object bound to the formal argument **argi** be a descendent of Ti'. Thus this conformance rule, which amounts to strengthening a precondition, is in conflict with the general philosophy about redefinition.

The last conformance rule has led to considerable controversy in the Eiffel community. We shall see, however, that there are many situations in which it seems to be quite appropriate.

We have seen that an assignment

```
x := y
```

is legal if the value of y is a descendent of the type of entity x. Up until now it appeared that creation

```
!!x
```

could only attach an object of the same type as x to entity x. There is, however, a generalization of the creation instruction:

```
! T !x
```

is a legal creation instruction if T is the name of a type conforming to the type of entity x. In this case an object of type T is created and bound to x.

We are now in a better position to understand what polymorphism is all about. Let us return to our example of a collection of employees. Suppose we have stored all the employees of our company in an array

```
workers : ARRAY [EMPLOYEE]
```

(An array is probably not the most suitable data structure for this purpose, but we won't go into that here.) In reality the elements stored in the array are likely to be very heterogeneous: there will be secretaries, salespeople, engineers and others among them. Nevertheless, at the end of the month we can print the paychecks using the following simple loop:

```
i : INTEGER
e : EMPLOYEE


...

from
    i := workers.lower
until
    i > workers.upper
loop
    e := workers.item (i)
    print_paycheck (e.name, e.months_pay)
    i := i + 1
end
```

Here we have assumed there is a procedure

```
print_paycheck (name : STRING, amount : REAL)
```

somewhere in the surrounding class.

The monthly pay will be computed for many different sorts of employees and in very widely differing fashions, as we saw earlier. Nevertheless each object reacts in its characteristic way to the request months_pay and does the right thing. That is what polymorphism is all about.

We have seen that an assignment

```
x := exp
```

is only valid if the type of the expression **exp** conforms to the (declared) type of entity **x**. There are, however, occasionally situations where we would like to do an assignment even though the types are exactly the wrong way around.

As an example consider a procedure **retrieve** that retrieves objects from a file or database (that have presumably been stored with a procedure **store**). Let us suppose that the class containing the procedure **retrieve** also has an attribute

```
last_object : ANY
```

which **retrieve** binds to the last object retrieved. The type of **last_object** must be **ANY**, since **retrieve** cannot know in advance what the type of a retrieved object will be. (**ANY** is a class to which all classes conform, as we shall see shortly.) Then we might want to retrieve a figure stored in the file using code something like this:

```
db : DATABASE
f  : FIGURE


...


db.retrieve
f := db.last_object
```

The problem is that, although we 'know' that the object retrieved is a **FIGURE**, the assignment above is the wrong way round: **ANY** does not conform to **FIGURE**.

For dealing with such (exceptional) cases Eiffel provides the *assignment attempt*. In our example it would look as follows:

```
f ?= db.last_object
```

The meaning of this instruction is: if the actual (dynamic) type of **last_object** does in fact conform to the type of **f**, then the assignment is made in the usual way. In every other case **f** is made **void**.

Note that if the assignment cannot be made because the types are not conforming there is no exception. The left side of the assignment is merely **void**.

Assignment attempts are costly. They require a check at runtime to determine whether the types are conformant. For this reason one should only use an assignment attempt when there is no other way to handle the problem.

Example Suppose we want to copy all the objects that are figures out of a file into another file and skip all those that are not figures. One might do this with code something like the following:

```
db1, db2 : FILE
fig      : FIGURE
```

```
    ...
from
    db1.open ("grab_bag")
    db2.create ("figures")
until
    db1.end_of_file
loop
    db1.retrieve
    fig ?= db1.last_object

    if fig /= void then
        db2.store (fig)
    end
end

db1.close
db2.close
```

6.7   Abstract classes

Some classes are so abstract in nature that we cannot actually define some (or perhaps even any) of their routines. An example of such a class is our class **EMPLOYEE** above. There is no sensible way to define the months_pay routine for a completely general employee.

In such cases we make the routine deferred. The definition for procedures then looks as follows:

```
pname (arg1 : T1; ... ) is

    require
        -- here the preconditions

    deferred

    ensure
        -- here the postconditions

    end
```

And for functions:

```
fname (arg1 : T1; ... ) : T is

    require
        -- here the preconditions
```

```
deferred

ensure
    -- here the postconditions

end
```

We are still free to formulate pre- and postconditions to describe what the abstract routine is supposed to do. But where the body of the routine would normally be we simply write **deferred**.

A class that contains at least one deferred routine is itself a deferred class. The class text must then begin with

deferred class CNAME

Deferred classes have the property that no instances of these classes can ever be created. They are purely abstract and exist simply so that other classes may inherit from them.

A class in which no routine is deferred is called **effective**. Only effective classes may have a creation routine, since only effective classes have instances.

An effective class that inherits from a deferred class must provide an effective version of each deferred feature in the deferred parent. This is done by redefinition of the deferred features. Thus the class **SECRETARY** will inherit from **EMPLOYEE** and make **months_pay** effective by giving an effective redefinition of it.

Example A good example for the use of abstract classes is the class **COMPARABLE** that defines the concept of a totally ordered set. It looks as follows:

deferred class COMPARABLE

feature

```
    infix "<" (other : like current) : BOOLEAN is

        deferred
        end
    --------------------------------------------------------

    infix ">" (other : like current) : BOOLEAN is

        do
            result := ( other < current )
        end
    --------------------------------------------------------
```

```
    infix "<=" (other : like current) : BOOLEAN is

        do
            result := not ( other < current )
        end
-----------------------------------------------------------

    infix ">=" (other : like current) : BOOLEAN is

        do
            result := not ( current < other )
        end
-----------------------------------------------------------

    compare (other : like current) : INTEGER is
                -- -1 if current < other
                --  1 if current > other
                --  0 otherwise

        do
            if current < other then
                result := -1
            elseif other < current then
                result := 1
            end          -- else result := 0 by default
        end

end -- class COMPARABLE
```

Remarks   This class illustrates a number of different points.

- Not all the routines needed to be made deferred. In this case we were able to base all of the other routines on the single routine "<". Thus only this one routine needed to be deferred. An effective class that inherits from COMPARABLE will then only need to make "<" effective; it obtains the others 'for free'.

- This class also illustrates the use of the predefined formal argument current which is bound to the object that was asked to carry out the routine.

- The class also illustrates the use of anchored declaration using like. In this case we have required that the second argument other should always be of the same type as the first (current). Thus whenever a class C inherits from COMPARABLE we will automatically ensure that other is of type C.

Now any class that has a natural total order may inherit from COMPARABLE so as to obtain its operators <, >, <=, >= . One good example is the class STRING, in which the order is the lexicographical order on strings. The class text for STRING might, in part, look as follows:

```
class STRING

inherit
    COMPARABLE
        redefine "<"
        end

feature

    infix "<" (other : like current) : BOOLEAN is

        external "C"
        alias "C_string_less"

        end

    ...

end -- class STRING
```

Two other classes that inherit from COMPARABLE are the basic classes INTEGER and REAL. They inherit simultaneously from an abstract class NUMERIC that provides the arithmetic operators

$$+, *, -, /, \char`\^$$

as well as the unary - and the neutral elements one, zero. Thus the class text for INTEGER will look something like the following:

```
class INTEGER

inherit
    COMPARABLE
        redefine
            infix "<"
        end;

    NUMERIC
        redefine
            infix "+", infix "-", infix "*", infix "/", infix "^",
            one, zero
        end
```

```
feature

    ...

end -- class INTEGER
```

Here we see a very natural use of multiple inheritance. If we had put the comparison operators `<`, `>`, `<=`, `>=` into the class `NUMERIC`, then we could have used single inheritance for the class `INTEGER` but we could not have allowed the class `STRING` to acquire its comparison operators by inheritance – at least not from `NUMERIC` since the operators `+`, `-`, `...` do not make sense for strings.

In Chapter 8 we shall give a very important reason why it is necessary for classes such as `STRING` to inherit from a class such as `COMPARABLE`, i.e. for them to conform to `COMPARABLE`. This has to do with constrained genericity.

We hope the reader noted that deferred routines may be provided with pre- and postconditions. These are used to formulate what the routine must do when it is made effective. Since these assertions are inherited by the effective version, they can help to enforce the intended semantics.

6.8   The inheritance graph

The classes of an Eiffel *universe* form a directed graph. The nodes of the graph are the classes and there is a directed edge from class `B` to class `A` if and only if `B` inherits directly from `A`, i.e. `A` is a parent of `B`.

This graph is required to be *acyclic*. In particular, it is not valid for `A` to inherit from `B` and `B` from `A`. But cycles passing through several classes in the inheritance relation are also forbidden.

The relation 'A is ancestor of B' can also be expressed in terms of the inheritance graph: it means that there is a directed path from `B` to `A` in the graph (there may be more than one).

There are four predefined classes that are always in the inheritance graph of every universe and every system. These are the classes

```
   GENERAL, PLATFORM, ANY, NONE
```

`PLATFORM` inherits from `GENERAL` and `ANY` from `PLATFORM`. Every other class in the universe that does not have an explicit `inherit` clause automatically inherits from `ANY`.

The class `NONE` is actually a fictional class (there is no class text for `NONE`), which may be thought of as inheriting from *every* other non-basic class. One must think of `NONE` as renaming every feature it inherits so as to avoid name clashes and as exporting no features at all. There is a feature

```
   void : NONE
```

in the class GENERAL and one may think of this as being the object referred to in such expressions as

    x = void

or assignments

    x := void

Since NONE inherits from every other non-basic class, void conforms to every such entity and thus such expressions and assignments as those above are always valid.

The class GENERAL contains a number of routines that are needed in every class. We will come back to them in a moment. The class PLATFORM contains any information that may be platform-dependent. Currently, it only contains the constants

    Boolean_bits, Character_bits, Integer_bits, Real_bits

which tell how many bits an object of the corresponding kind occupies on the local platform.

The class ANY adds no new features to those inherited from PLATFORM but can be used to define features needed by all classes in a project or company.

The routines defined in GENERAL are

```
equal (some : ANY; other : like some) : BOOLEAN
is_equal (other : like current) : BOOLEAN
clone (other : ANY) : like other
copy (other : like current)
deep_equal (some : ANY; other : like some) : BOOLEAN
deep_clone (other : ANY) : like other
deep_copy (other : like current)
conforms_to (other : ANY) : BOOLEAN
```

The function equal tests its two arguments field by field for equality. That is, it yields true if and only if the two objects are of the same dynamic type and their attributes have the same value pairwise (same in the sense of =). Note that the (invisible) argument current plays no role in equal except in cases when equal has been redefined. In that case one must write x.equal (a, b) in order to ensure that the version of equal from the class of x is used.

The function is_equal is similar to equal except that here other and current are compared with one another.

The function clone returns an exact copy of its argument other. That is, the result is a new object, but its attributes refer to the same objects as those of other.

The procedure copy is similar to clone except that it copies all of the attributes of other on to those of current. Thus

```
x := clone (y)
```

is equivalent to

```
!!x
x.copy (y)
```

The four routines just discussed only go to a depth of 1. They do not compare or copy the attributes of their arguments recursively. That is the task of the routines with **deep** in their names. They are recursive (and thus are correspondingly expensive).

Finally, the expression

```
x.conforms_to (y)
```

will yield **true** if and only if x is currently bound to an object of a type T which conforms to the declared (static) type of y. Thus the assignment

```
y := x
```

is only valid if x.conforms_to (y) yields **true**.

6.9   A calculator

We conclude this chapter with an example that illustrates the use of inheritance. We will show the basic steps in constructing a 'desk calculator' capable of evaluating arbitrarily complex expressions involving real numbers and the basic arithmetic operations +, -, * and /. An example of such an expression is

```
3.1 + 4.2 * (1.5 * 3.3 - 13.4) / 2.2
```

We want the usual precedence rules for these arithmetic operators to hold so that an expression such as

```
3.3 + 4.2 * 7.112
```

is interpreted as

```
3.3 + (4.2 * 7.112)
```

and not as

```
(3.3 + 4.2) * 7.112
```

This is a requirement made on the so-called 'parser' of our calculator; this is the part that analyzes the structure of an expression before it is evaluated.

The syntax of formal languages like that of our simple expressions is often formulated in a notation called EBNF (Extended Backus-Naur Form). The EBNF description of our arithmetic expressions could be formulated as follows:

```
expr ::= term { ('+' | '-') term } .
term ::= fact { ('*' | '/') fact } .
fact ::= const | '(' expr ')' .
```

The EBNF notation uses the symbol | to separate alternatives and the curly braces to mean zero or more occurences of the syntactical construct inside the braces. Thus the first of our rules states that an expression is either a single term or else a term followed by arbitrarily many constructs of the form

```
    + term
or  - term
```

This makes it possible to have arbitrarily long 'sums' such as

```
    term1 + term2 - term3 + term4 + ...
```

The rule defining the concept 'term' is very similar. It says a term is either a single factor or else a factor followed by arbitrarily many constructs of the form

```
    * factor
or  / factor
```

Hence a term can be an arbitrarily long 'product' such as

```
    fact1 * fact2 / fact3 * fact4 / ...
```

Finally, the third rule says that a factor is either a constant, which in our language will mean a real constant such as

```
    3.14159
```

or else it can be an arbitrary expression enclosed in parentheses.

The reader is invited to reflect upon why our breaking up the definition of expression in this way using terms and factors will indeed lead to the usual precedence rules for the arithmetic operators.

We will use four classes EXPRESSION, TERM, FACTOR and CONSTANT. Each of them will have the routine

```
    parse (s : SCANNER)
```

and since terms, factors and constants are particular kinds of expressions, the corresponding classes TERM, FACTOR and CONSTANT will inherit from EXPRESSION and will redefine this routine in a way appropriate for these sorts of expression.

The routine **parse** takes as argument an object of type SCANNER. We will discuss this class in a moment; a scanner has the task of taking an input stream of characters and breaking it up into syntactically useful chunks (called 'tokens') such as 'number', 'plus operator', 'left parenthesis', etc. Among other chores the scanner will eliminate blanks.

The routine **parse** can then ask the scanner to give it these chunks or tokens one after another and try to analyze the structure of the expression it is being given. If the analysis is successful (i.e. if the sequence of tokens did indeed represent a valid arithmetic expression), the routine `parse` calculates the value of the expression it found 'on the fly' and remembers this value with the attribute `value`. Otherwise, it sets its attribute `fail` to `true` to indicate that the expression was not formed correctly.

Our routine `parse` will implement the curly braces of EBNF by using iteration and will be recursive where the EBNF rules are recursive (as in defining 'factor' with the help of 'expression'). We shall show some of the four classes given above shortly. But first we need to know how the tokens (the syntactical chunks) are to be represented and what features the class SCANNER provides. We define tokens to be integer constants as defined in the following class:

```
class TOKENS

feature

    Error             : INTEGER is unique
    Constant          : INTEGER is unique
    Left_parenthesis  : INTEGER is unique
    Right_parenthesis : INTEGER is unique
    Add               : INTEGER is unique
    Subtract          : INTEGER is unique
    Multiply          : INTEGER is unique
    Divide            : INTEGER is unique
    End_of_text       : INTEGER is unique

end -- class TOKENS
```

The class SCANNER then provides the following features for the use of the parsing routines:

```
    set_text (s : STRING)   -- Initialize with a string
                            -- hopefully representing an
                            -- arithmetic expression.
    token : INTEGER         -- The current token
    advance                 -- Move to the next token
    value : REAL            -- Value of a real constant;
                            -- valid if token = Constant
```

Armed with this information we can now readily understand the class EXPRESSION:

```
class EXPRESSION

inherit
    TOKENS
```

```
feature

    value  : REAL
    failed : BOOLEAN
------------------------------------------------------------------

    reset is

        do
            failed := false
        end
------------------------------------------------------------------

    parse (s : SCANNER) is

        local
            term  : TERM
            token : INTEGER

        do
            from
                !!term
                term.parse (s)
                value := term.value
                token := s.token
            until
                term.failed or else
                (token /= Add and then token /= Subtract)
            loop
                s.advance  -- eat the '+' or '-'
                term.parse (s)

                if token = Add then
                    value := value + term.value
                else
                    value := value - term.value
                end

                token := s.token
            end

            failed := term.failed
        end

end -- class EXPRESSION
```

The reader should readily recognize that the structure of the routine **parse** mirrors the structure of the EBNF rule for an expression precisely. First, it tries to parse a term. If it succeeds it looks to see if the next token is a plus or a minus. If not, parse concludes that it must be finished. Otherwise, it consumes the token for the plus or minus and proceeds to parse another term.

The class **TERM** is so similar to **EXPRESSION** that we can safely leave it as an exercise for the reader. We proceed to the class **FACTOR** because it is a little different, although its structure also follows directly from the EBNF rule for factors:

```
class FACTOR

inherit
    EXPRESSION
        redefine
            parse
        end

feature

    parse (s : SCANNER) is

        local
            const : CONSTANT
            expr  : EXPRESSION

        do
            if s.token = Constant then
                !!const
                const.parse (s)
                value  := const.value
                failed := const.failed
            elseif s.token = Left_parenthesis then
                s.advance        -- eat the '('
                !!expr
                expr.parse (s)
                value  := expr.value
                failed := expr.failed

                if not failed            and then
                   s.token = Right_parenthesis then
                     s.advance   -- eat the ')'
                else
                     failed := true
                end
```

```
            else
                 failed := true
            end
        end

end -- class FACTOR
```

The class CONSTANT is quite simple; here it is:

```
class CONSTANT

inherit
    EXPRESSION
        redefine
            parse
        end

feature

    parse (s : SCANNER) is

        do
            value := s.value
            s.advance
        end

end -- class CONSTANT
```

To complete our calculator we now need the class **SCANNER**. This class is left to the reader as an exercise, since it does not illustrate any characteristic features of object-oriented programming. Finally, we need a root class to accept input from the user, parse it, evaluate the result and print the answer. The creation procedure of the root class will typically have a loop something like the following:

```
scan : SCANNER
expr : EXPRESSION
done : BOOLEAN

...
from
    !!scan.make
    !!expr
until
    done
loop
    get_a_string ("> ")
```

```
            if the_string.count = 0 then
                done := true
            else
                scan.set_text (the_string)
                expr.reset
                expr.parse (scan)

                if expr.failed then
                    put_a_string ("Bad expression%N")
                else
                    put_a_real (expr.value)
                    put_a_newline

                    if not scan.token = End_of_text then
                        put_a_string ("Extra characters in line%N")
                    end
                end
            end
        end
    end
```

We have assumed the existence of routines such as **get_a_string** and **put_a_real** for doing input and output. Either these will be defined in the root class or (more likely) they will be inherited from some standard class for performing this kind of task.

6.10   Exercises

1. In Ex. 3 of Chapter 4 you constructed a class **SET** that imitated the class **LIST**. Instead of making **SET** imitate **LIST**, let it inherit from **LIST**, providing only the features that are new in **SET**. Is this a good solution?

2. Rewrite your class **RATIONAL** from Ex. 1 in Chapter 4 so that it inherits from the classes **NUMERIC** and **COMPARABLE** and redefines the arithmetic and comparison operators. Do you see any advantage in this change?

3. Program the class **SCANNER** needed by the calculator described in the last section. The public interface of this class was given there. It will have the chore of taking the string given by **set_text** and breaking it up into a sequence of tokens as defined in the class **TOKENS**. If it finds anything in the string that cannot be interpreted as such a token, it must produce the token **Error**. When it reaches the end of the string, it must produce the token **End_of_text**.

   Your scanner will need to be able to turn a string of digits (and possibly a decimal point) into a real number. If you have Eiffel/S you should investigate the library class **FORMAT**. If you have some other Eiffel implementation there is likely to be a similar class for doing conversions from strings to numbers and back again.

4. Our calculator, as shown, does not handle the unary minus properly. For example, it will say that

```
1.0 + -2.0
```

is a 'Bad expression'. One could play tricks with the scanner to solve the problem but a cleaner solution is to redefine the grammar as follows. We rename our construct 'factor' as 'simple factor' and then introduce a new construct 'factor' with the rule

```
fact ::= simp | '-' simp .
```

Modify the calculator classes accordingly and try out the new version.

5. Our calculator does a very poor job of handling errors; it merely says 'Bad expression'. A good parser ought to give a much more helpful description of the error so that the user can find and repair it more easily. Try to make your calculator do a better job of error handling.

If you have Eiffel/S you should take a look at the class EXCEPTION and, in particular, at the procedure **raise**. By judicious use of this procedure you can avoid having all classes print messages to the console with **put_a_string** or the like. Instead, they simply raise an appropriate exception and leave it to some higher level class – probably the root class – to tell the user what has happened.

6. Our calculator also makes no attempt whatever to deal with semantic errors such as overflow on division; that is, if you divide a very large number by a very small number, a divide overflow will occur and the calculator will die with an exception. Try to make your calculator robust with respect to this kind of error by looking at the Eiffel/S class EXCEPT and then building appropriate **rescue** clauses.

Chapter 7

Repeated Inheritance

7.1   Some problems

This chapter deals with some complications that can arise through the use of
multiple inheritance. The reader may want to skip to the next chapter on a first
reading.

Since a class is allowed to inherit from several other classes there is no a priori
reason why it should not inherit from the *same* class several times. In fact, Eiffel
allows just that; it is called **repeated inheritance**.

Example

```
class B

inherit
    A; A

feature

    ...

end -- class B
```

Now it appears that here we have massive name clashes. Every feature of A seems
to cause a name clash. This is not so, however, because in fact a name clash only
occurs when two *different* features have the same name. Here the two 'versions'
of a feature f in A are indeed the *same* feature, and thus no name clash occurs.
(In fact, repeated inheritance in the naïve form just shown would be pointless;
the new class B is identical to the class we obtain if we leave out the second 'A'.)

One typical situation in which repeated inheritance is often used is the following. It frequently happens that one wishes to redefine a routine in a child
class, but the new routine is supposed to do what the old routine did and then

something more. One could of course copy the code of the old routine into the new routine. But why not just call the old routine first?

The problem with this idea is that the old routine is no longer 'visible' in the child class because its name has been claimed for the redefined version in the **inherit** clause. If one could rename the old routine first before redefining it, then one could have both the old and the new versions available at once. However, it is not permissible to rename and redefine a routine 'in the same breath', i.e. not in the same parent clause. This is a situation where one uses repeated inheritance.

Example

```
class B

inherit
    A
        rename
            make as A_make
        end;

    A
        redefine
            make
        select
            make
        end

creation
    make

feature

    make is

        do
            A_make     -- do old make first
            ...        -- then the new stuff
        end

    ...

end -- class B
```

The matter of name clashes needs a more thorough treatment. Let us first remark that the kind of repeated inheritance shown above is a **direct** repeated

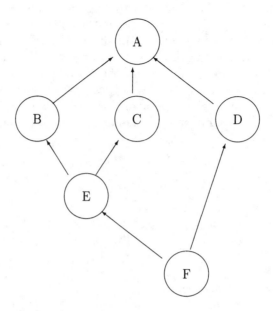

Figure 7.1 An inheritance graph

inheritance. **Indirect** repeated inheritance arises from the fact that the parent/child relations between classes do not form a tree as in simple inheritance but, rather, a directed acyclic graph (DAG). Thus there are in general several paths from a class to any of its ancestors.

Example Suppose classes B, C and D inherit from class A; E inherits from both B and C; and class F inherits from both D and E (see Fig. 7.1). Then there are three distinct paths from A to F:

$$A \to B \to E \to F \qquad A \to C \to E \to F \qquad A \to D \to F$$

On each of these three paths various features of A could be renamed or redefined, maybe even twice. Thus we need to know when a feature f of A ends up as several different features of F and when it stays as just one feature.

In what follows we shall need some definitions. The **signature** of a routine is as follows:

- the name of the routine,
- the number n of formal arguments (the predefined argument current is not counted),
- the types T1, T2, ..., Tn of the formal arguments,
- the return type T if the routine is a function.

Next we define the **origin** and **seed** of an effective feature f in a class D:

- If f is not inherited from any parent of D or if f is inherited from a deferred feature of a parent, then D is the origin of f and f is its own seed.
- If f is inherited from an effective feature g in a parent C of D, then the origin and seed of f are those of g.

Example Suppose that there is a function h in the class A in our diagram above and that it is introduced for the first time in this class. Suppose, further, that h is redefined in the descendent B and renamed to g in C. Then the class D will have two functions h and g (supposing no further renaming takes place between B and D or C and D). These two functions have the common seed h in the class A and A is the origin of these features.

Now let us consider the set of features in a newly defined class D: those defined explicitly in the class together with those inherited from all parents after application of renaming and redefinition. It can happen that two or more of these features have the same name f. We shall say that any two of them are **virtually the same** feature if:

- They are both effective and they have a common seed h in origin A and h was not redefined underway from A to D. In this case they are joined into one effective feature called f in D.
- They are both deferred and they have identical signature. In this case they are joined into one deferred feature called f in D.
- One of them is effective and one is deferred and they have identical signatures. In this case they are joined into one effective feature called f in D.

Name Clash Rule

We have a name clash in a class if two or more features have the same name and they are not virtually the same. The following table may help to clarify the situation:

	Same feature	Different feature
Same name	one feature	name clash
Different name	two features	two features

Let us illustrate this table using the example of the classes A, ..., F given earlier. The case 'same name/same feature' applies to a feature f in A that was neither renamed nor redefined on any path from A to F. This feature f results in one feature, also named f, in the class F.

The case 'same name/different feature' applies to a feature f in A that was redefined on at least one path from A to F but was never renamed. This produces a name clash. The name clash could also arise when new features that are both called h are introduced in, say, D and E.

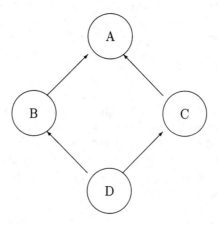

Figure 7.2 An inheritance graph

The case 'different name/same feature' applies to a feature **g** in **A** that is never redefined on any path from **A** to **F** but is renamed at least once – say to **h**. Then in **F** we have two distinct features with the names **g** and **h** that both stem from the **g** in **A**. The feature has been **split** or **replicated**.

If the feature **g** was a routine, then the question arises as to whether the code for this routine is duplicated in **F** or whether **g** and **h** are simply two names for the same code. This matter is left up to the compiler implementor.

Finally, we have the case 'different name/different feature'. This is the normal situation and, of course, leads to two distinct features in **F**.

7.2   The select clause

There is a situation in which multiple inheritance may lead to ambiguity about which routine is meant in an expression or instruction x.f. The following is an example of such a situation.

Example   Suppose that classes **B** and **C** inherit from class **A**, and class **D** inherits from both **B** and **C**. Further, suppose that **A** has a feature **f** that is redefined at least once on the way to **D** and is also renamed at least once (to avoid name clash). Then in **D** there are two distinct features that have seed **f** with origin **A**. Fig. 7.2 above illustrates this situation.

Now suppose that there is an entity

    x : A

in some class and in that class we have a call

    x.f

If at the moment when this call is carried out, the entity x is bound to an object of type D (which conforms to A), then it is not clear which of the two features with seed f is meant by this call. Such an ambiguity arises whenever we have a splitting of features of the sort described earlier. The select clause is introduced to resolve such ambiguities.

To stick to the example we were just considering, we show how the ambiguity would be resolved there:

```
class D

inherit
    B
        rename f as g
        end;

    C
        redefine f
        select f
        end

    ...

end -- class D
```

Here we have specified that the redefined version of f will be the one called by the call x.f above. We might have said select g instead. Then the other version would have been chosen.

A select clause is always needed in any situation where the splitting of a feature occurs.

7.3 Undefining a feature

It is possible to make an effective feature inherited from a parent into a deferred feature in the child. This is achieved by the undefine clause contained in the inherit clause. The undefine clause, if present, must follow the export (or rename) clause and precede the redefine clause:

```
class C

inherit
    A
        rename
            ...
        undefine
            f
```

```
      redefine
          ...
      end


   ...


end -- class C
```

This **undefine** clause may not necessarily lead to C having a deferred feature
(and thus being a deferred class). It could happen that an effective feature f
is inherited from another parent. According to the rules above, if both versions
of f have the same signature, then the result is a single effective feature named
f. Thus we have simply 'masked out' the one version of f to make the name
available for the other version.

7.4   Concluding remarks

The reader may by now have got the impression that multiple inheritance is
terribly complicated. Two things can be said about this:

- The examples given above are rather artificial and have been constructed
  to illustrate what *can* happen. Such complications are rare in practice.
- If the reader feels uneasy with multiple inheritance, no one will force him
  to use it. He can restrict himself exclusively to single inheritance and avoid
  the complications just described.

Chapter 8

Generic Classes

8.1 The problem

One of the greatest hindrances to writing reuseable software is the problem of variable types. The class COLLECTION, to which we referred several times in earlier chapters, is a good example of the kind of difficulties that arise here.

A COLLECTION is an abstract data type (ADT) representing a **container**, a thing into which objects of some fixed type can be put and in which they can be found again at some later time. The ADT has the following operations:

- add : stick an object into the container.
- remove : take an object out again.
- search : look to see if an object is in the container.
- found :   BOOLEAN : was the last search successful?
- count :   INTEGER : how many items are in the container now?

One could, for example, implement the ADT with an array that grows and shrinks dynamically as required or with a linked list or with any number of other data structures. In any case, the code is absolutely independent of the kind of object being kept in the collection. But in a strongly typed language we would nevertheless be compelled to make a different version of this class for every kind of object that we wanted to store in the collection: INTEGER_COLLECTION, VERTEX_COLLECTION, WINDOW_COLLECTION, etc.

What we need here is something like a parameterized family of types with a parameter that can specify the type of object being contained. Then we could write the code once and generate the type as required by choosing the right parameter. This is exactly what generic classes achieve.

8.2 Unconstrained genericity

In Chapter 1 we encountered one of the most frequently used generic classes: ARRAY. An array can hold a finite number of elements of some fixed type G. In

Eiffel we designate the type of the array for holding elements of type G with the notation

    ARRAY [G]

For each Eiffel type G we obtain a new type ARRAY [G]. Thus we may have

    ARRAY [INTEGER]

for arrays of integers and

    ARRAY [FIGURE]

for arrays of figures.

We spoke of using linked lists for implementing collections. In Chapter 4 we implemented linked lists; there we were forced to use an artificial class ELEMENT for the type of objects being stored in the list. Now we can reimplement our lists as a generic class:

```
class NODE [G]

feature

    item : G
    next : NODE [G]

---------------------------------------------------------

    set_item (x : G) is

        do
            item := x
        end
---------------------------------------------------------

    set_next (n : NODE [G]) is

        do
            next := n
        end

end -- class NODE


class LIST [G]

feature
```

```
    count : INTEGER

-----------------------------------------------------

    empty : BOOLEAN is

        do
            result := (count = 0)
        end
-----------------------------------------------------

    has (x : G) : BOOLEAN is

        local
            n : NODE [G]

        do
            from
                n := first
            until
                n = void or else equal (x, n.item)
            loop
                n := n.next
            end

            result := (n /= void)
        end
-----------------------------------------------------

    add (x : G) is

        local
            n : NODE [G]

        do
            if not has (x) then
                !!n
                n.set_item (x)
                n.set_next (first)
                first := n
                count := count + 1
            end
        end
-----------------------------------------------------
```

```
    remove (x : G) is

        local
            pre, post : NODE [G]

        do
            from
                pre := first
            until
                pre = void or else equal (x, pre.item)
            loop
                post := pre
                pre  := pre.next
            end

            if pre /= void then        -- found it!
                if first = void then -- was 1st node
                    first := pre.next
                else
                    post.set_next (pre.next)
                end

                count := count - 1
            end
        end
-----------------------------------------------------------


feature { NONE}

    first : NODE [G]

end -- class LIST
```

The general form of the **class** clause is

```
class CNAME [G1, G2, ..., Gk]
```

where G1, G2, ..., Gk are the generic parameters of the new class CNAME. And the name of a type has the form

```
    CNAME
```

or

```
    GCNAME [T1, T2, ..., Tn]
```

where CNAME is the name of a (non-generic) class and GCNAME is the name of a generic class with n generic parameters. T1, T2, ..., Tn are the names of n types. (Thus this definition is recursive.)

Examples

> ARRAY [ARRAY [VERTEX [REAL]]]
>
> TABLE [INTEGER, VERTEX [INTEGER]]

are two valid type names if we assume that VERTEX is a generic class with one generic parameter and that TABLE is a generic class with two generic parameters.

The example with the linked list above illustrates the meaning and use of the generic parameters in a generic class. Within the class text of a generic class the generic parameters can be used anywhere that a type name may otherwise be used:

- for declaring entities,
- as the return types of functions,
- as the types of formal arguments for routines,
- as the actual parameters in further type names.

An example of the last named use of generic parameters is in the following partial implementation of the class COLLECTION:

```
class COLLECTION [G]

creation
    make

feature

    count : INTEGER
    found : BOOLEAN


-----------------------------------------------------------


    make is

        do
            !!store.make (1, min_size)
        end
-----------------------------------------------------------

    add (x : G) is

        do
            if count = store.size then
                expand
            end
```

```
            count := count + 1
            store.put (x, count)
        end
```

        . . .

```
feature { NONE }

    min_size : INTEGER is 16
    store    : ARRAY [G]   -- here is where the elements are
```

```
end -- class COLLECTION
```

We do not regard a generic class as a class in the sense that we have been using so far. Instead, we shall think of a generic class as a **class germ**. It is a scheme or pattern for generating arbitrarily many actual classes. We obtain an actual class from such a class germ by substituting actual types for each of the generic parameters of the generic class. Thus COLLECTION [VERTEX [INTEGER]] is an actual class; VERTEX [INTEGER] is an actual type obtained from the class germ VERTEX by substituting the actual type INTEGER for the generic parameter. And thus we may substitute VERTEX [INTEGER] for the generic parameter of COLLECTION.

In the same spirit we must regard such declarations as

```
    store : ARRAY [G]   -- here is where the elements are
```

as being declarations of **entity germs**. The entity germ store becomes an actual entity only after substitution of an actual type for the parameter G. Thus in

```
    COLLECTION [VERTEX [INTEGER]]
```

we have an actual entity store of type

```
    ARRAY [VERTEX [INTEGER]].
```

The **inherit** clause of a generic class may contain other generic classes.

Example

```
class C [G]

inherit
    B [G]


    . . .


end -- class C
```

For generic classes we must formulate the parent/child relation as follows: if an actual class B arises from a generic class by substituting actual types for the generic parameters, then the parents of B are the actual classes that appear in the inherit clause after substitution of the actual parameters. In our example above, B [INTEGER] is a parent of C [INTEGER] but not of C [POINT]. And B [POINT] is a parent of C [POINT] but not of C [INTEGER].

Our definition of conformance in Chapter 5 was only a preliminary definition. We must now modify it somewhat to deal with generic classes. The complete definition is as follows.

Definition
A type B **conforms to** a type A if and only if one of the following holds:

1. A and B are the same type.
2. A is type C [S1, S2, ..., Sn] and B is type C [T1, T2, ..., Tn], where C [G1, G2, ..., Gn] is a generic class with n generic parameters and S1, ..., Sn, T1, ..., Tn are actual types such that Ti conforms to Si for $i = 1, \ldots, n$.
3. Some parent of B conforms to A.

Examples

(i) By Rule 2 the type

    TABLE [STRING, INTEGER]

conforms to the type

    TABLE [HASHABLE, NUMERIC]

since **STRING** conforms to HASHABLE and INTEGER to NUMERIC.

(ii) If the class text of HASH_TABLE begins like this:

```
class HASH_TABLE [K, G]

inherit
    TABLE [K, G]

...
```

then, by Rule 3 and Example (i), it follows that HASH_TABLE [STRING, INTEGER] conforms to TABLE [HASHABLE, NUMERIC]. This is true because TABLE [STRING, INTEGER] is a parent of HASH_TABLE [STRING, INTEGER].

The question of conformance only arises for actual classes (or types) since we never have instances of class germs – only instances of actual classes. Similarly, we never have entities with class germs as their type; actual entities have actual classes as their type.

8.3 Constrained genericity

What can one do with entity germs in a generic class (or class germ)? An
example is the entity `item` in our class `NODE` above. Since any type whatever may
be substituted for the generic parameter G, we may not make any assumptions
about what features the entity might have. Thus the simple expression

```
item
```

is the only expression that we can form with the entity `item`. And the only
permissible assignment to such an entity is one in which the expression on the
right is of type G, since this is the only kind of expression that can be guaranteed
to conform to `item`. An example occurs in the routine

```
set_item (x : G) is

    do
        item := x
    end
```

We may also make comparisons using = and /= but, again, only if the entity
being compared to `item` is also of type G.

This is a very restricted list of things that we are allowed to do with entity
germs. However, we are often in the situation of wanting to assume that our
entity germs have a minimal set of known features. A good example where
such assumptions are needed is in the class `SORTED_LIST`. Here we would like to
assume that the items have a total order, that is, they have at least a feature < .
We see that we often need some way of restricting or constraining the permissible
generic types to those that provide some prescribed set of features.

If we look again at the example of `SORTED_LIST`, we see that what we really
require is that the generic type conform to `COMPARABLE`. And, indeed, this is the
usual situation: we require the generic type to conform to some given type.

Eiffel therefore provides the notion of **constrained genericity**. This is expressed in the `class` clause as follows:

```
class C [G1 -> T1, G2 -> T2, ...]
```

This means that for `Gi` we are only allowed to substitute actual types that conform to the type `Ti`. The earlier notation for unconstrained genericity

```
class C [G]
```

can be understood as shorthand for

```
class C [G -> ANY]
```

At least that would be true if it weren't for the basic types. The class `ANY` is a
predefined class from which every non-basic class automatically inherits, as we
saw in Chapter 5.

Using constrained genericity we now have no problem in defining a class
`SORTED_LIST`. It might look something like the following:

```
class SORTED_LIST [G -> COMPARABLE]

feature

    count : INTEGER    -- how many nodes in list?
    found : BOOLEAN    -- was last search successful?
----------------------------------------------------------------

    add (x : G) is

        local
            m, n, p : like first

        do
            !!n.make (x)

            from
                m := first
            until
                m = void or else x < m.item
            loop
                p := m
                m := m.next
            end

            n.set_next(m)

            if p = void then
                first := n
            else
                p.set_next(n)
            end

            count := count + 1
        end

    ...


----------------------------------------------------------------

feature { NONE }

    first : NODE [G] -- reference to first node

end -- class SORTED_LIST
```

In the expression

```
m = void or else x < m.item
```

we have used the fact that objects of type G have a feature < . This is guaranteed by the constraint G -> COMPARABLE.

As a further illustration of constrained genericity we give an implementation of a class MATRIX. We want our matrices to have operations +, -, * so we constrain the type of entry in the matrix to conform to NUMERIC:

```
class MATRIX [G -> NUMERIC]

creation
    make

feature

    n_row : INTEGER
    n_col : INTEGER


-------------------------------------------------------------


    make (m, n : INTEGER) is

        require
            m > 0 and n > 0

        do
            n_row := m
            n_col := n
            !!store.make (1, m * n)
        end
-------------------------------------------------------------


    put (x : G; i, j : INTEGER) is

        require
            1 <= i and then i <= n_row
            1 <= j and then j <= n_col

        do
            store.put (x, (i - 1) * n_col + j)
        end
-------------------------------------------------------------
```

```
    item (i, j : INTEGER) : G is

        require
            1 <= i and then i <= n_row
            1 <= j and then j <= n_col

        do
            result := store.item ((i - 1) * n_col + j)
        end
```

```
    infix "*" (other : like current) : like current is

        require
            right_size : n_col = other.n_row
            non_void   : -- no entry is void

        local
            i, j, k : INTEGER
            entry   : G
            zero    : G

        do
            !!result.make (n_row, other.n_col)
            zero := item (1, 1).zero

            from
                i := 1
            until
                i > n_row
            loop
                from
                    j := 1
                until
                    j > other.n_col
                loop
                    from
                        entry := zero
                        k     := 1
                    until
                        k > n_col
                    loop
                        entry := entry +
                            item (i, k) * other.item (k, j)
```

```
                            k := k + 1
                    end

                    result.put (entry, i, j)
                    j := j + 1
                end

            i := i + 1
        end
    end

    ...
```

```
feature { NONE }

    store : ARRAY [G]

end -- class MATRIX
```

Remark One might be very tempted to let MATRIX inherit from NUMERIC and **redefine** the abstract operators +, -, *. This turns out to be a poor idea, however; for what should we do with the operation /? Furthermore, the feature **one** in NUMERIC cannot be defined sensibly for matrices. We would need a different version of **one** for every possible value of n_row.

8.4   Exercises

1. Modify your example class SET from Chapter 4 to make it a generic class SET [G].
2. If you have Eiffel/S, take a good look at the cluster CONTAIN, which has numerous classes for 'containing' arbitrary kinds of objects. Most of these classes are generic and serve nicely to illustrate the uses of generic classes.

Chapter 9

Libraries

9.1 Reusable components

At the NATO Conference on Software Engineering in Garmisch-Partenkirchen in 1968 Doug McIlroy formulated what eventually became one of the central goals of software engineering: the ability to produce reusable software components. These components should be so carefully constructed and 'normed' that one could 'take them off the shelf', so to speak, and insert them into a new piece of software wherever they might be needed without having to make a single change in them.

Of course, it is not true that there were no libraries of reusable software available in 1968. There were in fact many such libraries. The following are some examples:

- Every operating system provides a collection of 'system calls' that any application programmer can use in order to acquire the services of the operating system. These can be used to create new files, write data into them, read it again, and so on.
- Many programming languages are routinely provided with a standard library of frequently needed functions or subroutines. Thus one has functions for manipulating strings, for the allocation and freeing of blocks of memory on the heap, for buffered input and output, etc.
- There is a very substantial library of mathematical functions written in FORTRAN.
- Likewise, there are libraries of routines with which one can undertake plotting.

But all of these libraries have the property that they are collections of individual *functions* or *procedures*. If one looks for reusable *data structures*, one does not find much. At least that was the case until the object-oriented languages appeared on the scene.

The builder of a compiler would like to be able to take a complete symbol table out of his work box and stick it into his new compiler without having to make any alterations to it. And how often one programs queues for various purposes in ever new variations! One can seldom take the queues that one has programmed for some other application because they were made to accept some data type that was special to that application.

9.2   The problems

Let us look first at the problems faced by someone wishing to provide a library of reusable data structures. To illustrate the problems we consider the concrete case of a `Dictionary`. This is an abstract data type with the following operations and axioms:

```
Operations:
    has (k : KEY) : BOOLEAN  -- Is something stored under
                             -- the key k?
    at (k : KEY) : INFO      -- What is stored there?
                             -- Precondition: has (k)
    put (x : INFO; k : KEY)  -- Make x the info stored
                             -- under key k.

Axioms:
i)      after put (x, k) we have has (k)
ii)     after put (x, k) we have at (k) = x
```

A `Dictionary` is also often called an *associative array*. It has largely the same semantics as an array except that the indices are not necessarily integers. They can be of some arbitrary type.

The following are the problems that need to be solved:

1. How can one implement such an abstract data type? That is, how can one provide a data structure together with the appropriate operations?
2. How can one make the preconditions of partial functions such as `at` visible to the user of the abstract data type? Even better would be to have the system check at runtime that the preconditions are not violated.
3. In our example above, the fictitious types `INFO` and `KEY` were used but stood for some quite arbitrary type. How can we leave such *parameters* open to be specified later by the users of the ADT?
4. Suppose a potential user of our ADT `Dictionary` finds that it almost suits her needs except that she also needs to be able to remove elements from the dictionary. Can the ADT be extended with further properties and operations without affecting the software that already uses it?

5. Can the library of data structures provide a reliable, flexible and uniform treatment of errors? 'Reliable' means that no error goes unrepaired and unreported. 'Flexible' means that the libraries provide *mechanisms* for dealing with errors but do not specify *policies*. For example, it would generally not be acceptable if such a reusable library wrote its own error messages to the console screen.

   'Uniform' means that if a program uses two different libraries, I and II, it does not need to have two distinct error handling routines: one to deal with errors arising in library I and the other for errors arising in library II.

The reader, of course, knows how these questions can be answered using Eiffel:

1. The abstract data types are implemented using classes. The properties and operations of a data type are represented by the attributes and routines of the class.
2. The preconditions of partial functions and routines can be formulated in Eiffel. If they can be formulated as Boolean expressions, they can be checked at runtime.
3. Parameterized types are no problem. These are realized in Eiffel using generic classes.
4. Extending or modifying already existing ADTs is also no problem in an object-oriented language. One creates a new class that inherits from the existing one and adds only the new features needed, or redefines those that are needed in a new form. Thus the ADT `Dictionary` above could be extended by creating a new class `REM_DICTIONARY` that inherits from `DICTIONARY` and adds just the one routine `remove`. Existing software that uses the class `DICTIONARY` is in no way affected.
5. The requirement of reliable, flexible and uniform error handling is fulfilled by the Eiffel exception mechanism. Reusable library classes should pass to their callers any exception conditions that cannot be repaired on the spot. Then each application program can deal with errors in its own style.

The problems discussed so far must be solved before reusable ADTs even become possible. In Eiffel they have been solved in quite a satisfactory manner. The following group of problems only becomes acute once the technology of reusable libraries becomes successful and widespread:

1. How should the different ADTs be organized? ADTs seldom come alone; usually they form families or *clusters* of related abstractions. Thus we might have such clusters as `FIGURE`, `CIRCLE`, `ELLIPSE`, etc., or `LIST`, `LIST_NODE`, `TREE`, etc.
2. How can name clashes be avoided? If the technology of reusable software is successful, then it is quite likely that a project will use libraries from different sources. A library of general data structures could have a class `NODE` (nodes for linked lists). Another library from a different source that

deals with network communication could also have a class NODE (a node
in a communication network). But in any given program the class names
must be unique.

3. How can the programmer find out what abstractions are available and how
to use them?

The first of these problems has a simple solution under most operating systems:
put all classes that belong to one cluster into a directory named for the cluster.
That, however, is only the beginning of a solution. The programmer using these
libraries to construct a new program needs a tool with which he can describe
which clusters will be needed in his new project and where they can be found.

This is a point at which various Eiffel implementations begin to diverge from
one another. We shall look at the solution offered by Eiffel/S; other Eiffel implementations have a similar solution.

In a Program Description File (called xyz.pdl if the program is called xyz),
the programmer describes the program to be built. This includes giving the
name of the program, the name of the root class and the creation procedure in
the root class to be called when the program starts. This might look as follows:

```
program word_count

root
    wordref : "make"


...
```

Here the program is to be called word_count and the root class is WORDREF. The
creation procedure to be used is make.

More important, however, is the information about the clusters to be used.
The Program Description File can (and should) include a cluster clause that
will look something like this:

```
cluster

    "./"
    end

    "$EIFFEL_S/library/basic"
    end

    "$EIFFEL_S/library/contain"
    end

    "$EIFFEL_S/library/math"
    end
```

This clause tells the Eiffel compiler that four clusters will be needed and where they can be found, i.e. the paths to the corresponding directories. In this case the current working directory contains one of the clusters (these are the classes being developed especially for the new application). The other three clusters are standard library clusters delivered with Eiffel/S: the basic cluster, the container cluster and the math cluster.

The second problem mentioned above is that of name clashes between clusters from different sources. This problem can also be solved using the Program Description File. The `cluster` clause can be much more complicated than that shown in the example above.

Example Let us consider again our earlier example with the two classes named NODE. In principle, one could solve this problem by changing the name of one of the two classes and altering all references to this class in all classes of the corresponding cluster. A moment's reflection, however, shows that this is a very poor solution – for the same reasons that we gave in connection with name clashes caused by multiple inheritance. It could be that both of the clusters involved in the name clash have been used in other software projects (although never both in the same project until now). Altering either of them in the way just described would invalidate those projects.

Using the Program Description File we can solve this problem in a way that is very reminiscent of the way name clashes caused by multiple inheritance were solved:

```
cluster

    "."
    end

    "local/library/network"
        rename
            NODE as NET_NODE
        use
            NET_NODE for all
    end
```

Here the Program Description File is telling the Eiffel compiler that, for this project (and only for this one), the class NODE from the network cluster is to be renamed NET_NODE. Moreover, all references to NODE in that cluster are to be replaced by references to NET_NODE. The compiler makes these replacements internally; the class texts are not altered physically. Thus other projects are not affected by this renaming procedure.

An additional problem with the mapping of classes to files stems from the fact that many operating systems limit the lengths of file names. Classes would often have cryptic names if we were restricted to choosing names that were no longer than the maximum length of a file name. To avoid this inconvenience the `cluster` clause in the Program Description File allows a subclause of the following type:

```
find
    exception_handler in "x_hdlr.e",
    overdraw_handler  in "o_hdlr.e",
    ...
```

Here the compiler is being told that the class `EXCEPTION_HANDLER` is not to be sought in a file with name `exception_handler.e` but, rather, in `x_hdlr.e`. Under an operating system such as MS-DOS, which only allows file names to be at most eight characters long, the `find` clauses are likely to be lengthy.

The last of the problems mentioned was the question of how a programmer can find out what abstract data types are available and how to use them. If the reusable software technology is very successful, this will be an especially important question. As long as there are only half a dozen clusters available, a programmer might be expected to use printed documentation to inform herself about them. When there are many dozens of such clusters available, any viable solution must involve online help.

The solution in the long run will undoubtedly make use of a database with a suitable query language. If, for example, a programmer needs a class representing a binomial probability distribution, he will query the database with a keyword such as 'probability' to find out whether such a thing is available or whether he must program it himself.

At present, none of the commercially available object-oriented programming languages offers anything like this database. The best that Eiffel currently offers in this direction is the `indexing` clause, which has the form

```
indexing
    list of keywords
```

and must appear at the beginning of a class text. The Eiffel compiler simply ignores this clause; it is intended for some other tool that manages classification or cross-referencing of Eiffel classes. If such a database as the one described above should be created for Eiffel someday, then there would need to be a universal convention about the information in an `indexing` clause, for otherwise it would not do anyone much good.

9.3   Some Eiffel libraries

As we mentioned in the preface at the time of writing this book there was only one implementation of Eiffel 3 available, Eiffel/S. The libraries provided with Eiffel/S differ from those provided with Interactive Software's implementation of Eiffel 2 (and from those described in [Ref. 2]). But to build some real programs we will need some library classes for Eiffel 3, so in what follows we use those of Eiffel/S.

We shall not look at all the clusters that belong to the Eiffel/S library. Some of them will be used in the chapters that follow and will be discussed when they are needed. We conclude this chapter by looking at some of the most important classes in the cluster basic.

The cluster basic includes all classes that are intimately connected with the language Eiffel such as the basic classes BOOLEAN, CHARACTER, INTEGER, REAL. It also includes ARRAY and STRING, as well as those classes from which these fundamental classes inherit: COMPARABLE, NUMERIC and HASHABLE. It must also include the classes from which all other classes inherit, the ones at the top of the inheritance graph described in Chapter 6: GENERAL, PLATFORM and ANY. We do not need to say anything more about any of these classes.

More interesting is the class EXCEPTION, which permits 'fine tuning' of the exception mechanism. In Chapter 5 we learned that the Eiffel runtime system raises an exception if assertion checking is turned on and an assertion is violated. It also raises an exception if any operation involving the operating system (such as reading or writing files) causes an error. But we did not see any way in which an ordinary Eiffel class could raise an exception if some other error occurred. That is where the class EXCEPTION comes in.

The most important feature of the class EXCEPTION is

```
raise (routine_name : STRING,
       message       : STRING,
       code          : INTEGER,
       xobject       : ANY     )
```

which can be called wherever an exception must be raised. The first argument should be the name of the routine in which the error occurs. The second is a string describing the error, and the third is an integer code that should also specify the error uniquely. The fourth argument can be any Eiffel object and allows a very flexible treatment of errors.

Further important features of the class EXCEPTION are the attributes

```
last_ecall : STRING
last_etext : STRING
last_ecode : INTEGER
last_eobj  : ANY
```

which only have meaningful values after an exception has been raised, and correspond in an obvious fashion to the arguments with which raise was called. Thus these attributes should only be accessed in a rescue clause, because that is the only place where one can be sure that they have significant values.

There are two typical styles for dealing with exceptions:

1. One can define a new exception class by inheriting from EXCEPTION and introducing special exception codes suitable for the application being developed. This might look as follows:

```
class OUR_EXCEPTION

inherit
    EXCEPTION

feature

    OUT_OF_RANGE : INTEGER is 1
    TOO_MANY     : INTEGER is 2
    OVERDRAWN    : INTEGER is 3
    ...

end -- class OUR_EXCEPTION
```

Then one uses these codes when raising exceptions and sets the fourth argument equal to **void**. The **rescue** clauses will then typically contain multibranch instructions such as the following:

```
rescue
    inspect last_ecode

    when OUT_OF_RANGE then
        ...

    when TOO_MANY then
        ...

    when OVERDRAWN then
        ...

    end
end
```

2. Alternatively, one can define an abstract exception handler class as follows:

```
deferred class EXCEPTION_HANDLER

feature

    handle is

        deferred
        end

end -- class EXCEPTION_HANDLER
```

For each kind of exception that can occur, one derives an appropriate effective class from EXCEPTION_HANDLER with a suitable redefinition of handle. Raising an exception might then look as follows:

```
local
     o_hdlr : OVERDRAW_HANDLER


    ...


if overdrawn then
    !!o_hdlr
    raise ("acc.withdraw",
            "Account overdrawn",
            0, o_hdlr            )
end
```

With this method the rescue clause is always very simple. It might look something like the following:

```
some_routine is

    local
         xhdlr : EXCEPTION_HANDLER

    do

        ...

    rescue
         xhdlr ?= last_eobj

         if xhdlr /= void then
             xhdlr.handle
         end
    end
```

Another very useful class in the cluster basic is ENVIRONMENT, which gives an Eiffel program access to the command line with which the program was executed by the user as well as to the environment variables that the operating system makes available. A typical use of this class looks as follows:

```
if arg_count > 0 then
    path := arg_item (1)
else
    get_a_string ("Input file : ")
    path := the_string
end
```

Here the program first checks to see if there was at least one component in the command line (other than the name of the program to be executed). The feature `arg_count` in ENVIRONMENT is the number of components in the command line. If this number is positive it assumes that the first such component is the path of a file to be used. The function `arg_item` in the class ENVIRONMENT behaves like an array of strings and returns the components of the command line. If the command line was empty the program requests the name of the path from the user.

Another cluster that we shall often need is `contain`. It provides various 'container' classes in which objects can be stored and retrieved: lists, tables, queues, stacks, dictionaries, catalogs. But we shall describe these classes at the points where we actually need them. In the following chapters we look at some examples of Eiffel programs.

Chapter 10

A Library Manager

10.1 A substantial example

So far, we have made the acquaintance of many constructs of the language Eiffel, but have only seen fragments of Eiffel classes. It is time to take a look at a complete Eiffel program in order to see how one typically uses an object-oriented language like Eiffel.

The example program presented in this chapter illustrates nicely how reusable library classes can make the programmer's life easier. The program does not, however, have a style or structure typical of truly object-oriented programs. Its style is not very different from that of a program that one might write in Pascal or C. In the next chapter we shall see a program that has a distinctly object-oriented flavor.

10.2 A library manager

The task we set ourselves here is to create a manager for a personal library. Our manager is to keep track of all the books belonging to the library, along with their titles, authors and catalog numbers (ISBN). It must also record which books have been borrowed by whom and when they are due to be returned. It must be able to answer such questions as: 'Which books by author John Doe are in the library?' or: 'Which books does Jane Plain have checked out?'

I said this was a manager for a 'personal' library, because it handles everything in main memory. One could not do that with a 'real' library; a database would be more suitable in that case.

One of the first tasks in designing an object-oriented program is to find the right classes. One must ask oneself: 'What are the objects or materials that are to be manipulated or simulated here?' In our case we immediately think of three kinds of object: book, person, library. The category 'person' might be further specialized to 'author' and 'borrower'. Since, however, only the name of a person is ever used in our simple application, it soon becomes clear that there is no real point in having a separate category 'person', so we drop that potential class again. We are left with 'book' and 'library'.

10.3   The class BOOK

What properties of a book interest us here? The following list quickly comes to mind: ISBN, author, title, borrower, date due. One need not, of course, store the name of a borrower in the object representing the borrowed book. But if we look up a book and discover that it is on loan, it could be interesting to know who has it. If that information is not stored with the book, then we will have to search through the list of borrowers or some other list to find that information. So we decide to leave 'borrower' as one of the attributes of 'book'.

Given these properties of a book we shall clearly need the following operations for a book:

```
lend (borrower, date_due)
return
on_loan : BOOLEAN
```

as well as a creation procedure by which ISBN, title and author are specified.

Our class BOOK is now quickly implemented:

```
class BOOK

creation
    make

feature

    isbn     : STRING
    author   : STRING
    title    : STRING
    borrower : STRING
    date_due : REAL

----------------------------------------------------------

    make (new_isbn, new_author, new_title : STRING) is

        require
            good_isbn   : new_isbn /= void and then
                          new_isbn.count > 0
            good_author : new_author /= void and then
                          new_author.count > 0
```

```
        do
            isbn    := new_isbn
            author := new_author
            title  := new_title
        end
```

```
    lend (to_borrower : STRING; due : REAL) is

        require
            good_borrower : borrower /= void and then
                              borrower.count > 0

        do
            borrower := to_borrower
            date_due := due
        end
```

```
    return is

        do
            borrower := void
        end
```

```
    on_loan : BOOLEAN is

        do
            result := (borrower /= void)
        end

end -- class BOOK
```

Remarks

- One could have made on_loan a BOOLEAN attribute of BOOK. We have chosen to say that a book is on loan precisely when borrower is not void.
- Why is the catalog number isbn not an INTEGER? Because these 'numbers' can in fact contain letters.
- That date_due is a REAL is also rather surprising. The reason is that Eiffel/S treats time as a real number.

10.4 The class LIBRARY

The books were easy enough. Now we turn to the library. Again, it is important
to think about the operations we will want to carry out with our library. Let's
try to collect them first:

```
add_book (isbn, author, title : STRING)
find_with_isbn (isbn : STRING) : BOOK
find_with_author (author : STRING) : LIST [BOOK]
borrowed (borrower : STRING) : LIST [BOOK]
lend (isbn, borrower : STRING; date_due : REAL)
return (isbn : STRING)
overdue : LIST [BOOK]
```

Some of these operations are obvious, given the tasks of our library manager
mentioned above: adding new books to the library, lending and returning books,
and answering questions about books. Somewhat less obvious is the operation
find_with_isbn. However, we shall find this operation useful when we program
our actual library manager.

The result of the queries find_with_author and borrowed will in general not
just be a single book but, rather, a whole list of books. For this reason we have
given the type of the return value as LIST [BOOK]. We hope, of course, that there
is such a class already in a suitable library. If not, we shall have to program one.

How should we organize the books in our library so as to be able to carry out
the above operations as efficiently as possible? In particular, we shall stipulate
that answering the queries find_with_author and borrowed should be as fast
as possible. Here it turns out to be useful to think about how these tasks are
dealt with in a real library. If one wants to know which books a given author
has written, one looks in a *catalog* under the author's name. There one finds a
number of cards with the titles and numbers of all books by the author that are
present in the library. So we need something like a catalog that can be queried
with the name of an author. The problem of finding all books borrowed by a
given user could be solved in the same way.

Now it is time to take a look into the Eiffel/S library to see what classes it can
offer us to assist in our project. In the cluster contain we find classes LIST and
CATALOG, so our task is already beginning to look easier. A closer look reveals
that, in addition to LIST, there are also classes SHORT_LIST and SORTED_LIST,
as well as SHORT_SORTED_LIST, so we are going to have to make some choices.

SORTED_LIST requires its elements to conform to COMPARABLE but then
promises to keep them sorted, which makes searching for a particular element
faster. This functionality does not seem to be necessary for our simple application and, besides, it's not clear what order relation one should take for the set
of all books. So let's leave sorted lists out of our considerations.

The Eiffel/S library manual reveals that SHORT_LIST has the same syntax and
semantics as LIST but is more frugal with memory – at the price of being slower
for some operations. It is recommended that SHORT_LIST be used when the lists

are expected to have, at most, a few dozen elements. This seems to be just what we want for the list of books written by one author and for the list of books borrowed by one user. So let's take short lists for these two situations. On the other hand, the list of all overdue books could conceivably be quite long. So we decide to let that be a LIST.

Now we look at the class CATALOG. It is a generic class

```
CATALOG [G, K -> HASHABLE]
```

where G is the type of the information stored with a key of type K. It provides features

```
add (x : G; key : K)
remove (x : G; key : K)
has (key : K) : BOOLEAN
at (key : K) : COLLECTION [G]
```

which seem to be just what we need. However, COLLECTION is an abstract (deferred) class and therefore CATALOG is also deferred. The effective descendents are SHORT_CATALOG, LIST_CATALOG, SORTED_CATALOG and SHORT_SORTED_CATALOG, reflecting the fact that the return type of at can be a SHORT_LIST, a LIST, a SORTED_LIST or a SHORT_SORTED_LIST. Thus we decide to use SHORT_CATALOG, one for the authors and one for the borrowers.

Catalogs are suitable for implementing one–many relations like author/title or borrower/book. However, our operation find_with_isbn will require us to maintain a one–one relation isbn/book. It seems silly to use a catalog for this purpose, because the 'list' of books that will be returned for a given catalog number will always have at most one element. Another look into the cluster contain turns up the class DICTIONARY, which is in fact just what we need. A dictionary has a syntax and semantics similar to that of catalog except that at returns a single element of type G instead of an entire collection.

Now we are in a good position to implement our class LIBRARY. The private attributes will be as follows:

```
feature { NONE }
```

```
shelf     : DICTIONARY [BOOK, STRING]
authors   : SHORT_CATALOG [BOOK, STRING]
borrowers : SHORT_CATALOG [BOOK, STRING]
```

Most of the routines in our class are now extremely simple to implement. They are as follows:

```
    make is

        do
            !!shelf.make
            !!authors.make
            !!borrowers.make
        end
```

```
    add_book (isbn, author, title : STRING) is

        require
            good_isbn   : isbn /= void and then
                             isbn.count > 0
            good_author : author /= void and then
                             author.count > 0

        local
            b : BOOK

        do
            !!b.make (isbn, author, title)
            shelf.put (b, isbn)
            authors.add (b, author)
        end
```

```
    find_with_isbn (isbn : STRING) : BOOK is

        require
            good_isbn : isbn /= void and then
                           isbn.count > 0

        do
            if shelf.has (isbn) then
                result := shelf.at (isbn)
            end
        end
```

```
    find_with_author (author : STRING) : SHORT_LIST [BOOK] is

        require
            good_author : author /= void and then
                             author.count > 0
```

```
        do
            if authors.has (author) then
                result := authors.at (author)
            end
        end
```

```
    borrowed (borrower : STRING) : SHORT_LIST [BOOK] is

        require
            good_borrower : borrower /= void and then
                            borrower.count > 0

        do
            if borrowers.has (borrower) then
                result := borrowers.at (borrower)
            end
        end
```

```
    lend (isbn, borrower : STRING; date_due : REAL) is

        require
            book_there     : shelf.has (isbn)
            book_available : not shelf.at (isbn).on_loan
            good_borrower  : borrower /= void and then
                             borrower.count > 0

        local
            bk : BOOK

        do
            bk := shelf.at (isbn)
            bk.lend (borrower, date_due)
            borrowers.add (bk, borrower)
        end
```

```
    return (isbn : STRING) is

        require
            book_there  : shelf.has (isbn)
            book_loaned : shelf.at (isbn).on_loan
```

```
local
    bk : BOOK

do
    bk := shelf.at (isbn)
    borrowers.remove (bk, bk.borrower)
    bk.return
end
```

The only routine that is a little more complicated is **overdue**. It must go through the entire catalog of all borrowers and look at all the books entered there to see if their date due is earlier than today's date. We'll look at the problem of finding out today's date in just a moment. First, though, we want to see how one can traverse all entries in a catalog (or other container for that matter).

For this purpose the Eiffel/S library provides the abstraction 'iterator'. An iterator can traverse all elements of any container object that is a descendent of **TRAVERSABLE**. This includes **CATALOG** and its descendents, so obviously an iterator is just what we need.

Any descendent of **TRAVERSABLE** has a function

```
iterator : ITERATOR
```

which returns an object of type **ITERATOR** that is prepared to traverse the given container. One can have arbitrarily many such iterators traversing the same container at once. They are independent of one another and do not interfere with each other.

The class **ITERATOR** has the following features:

```
first    -- go to first item
forth    -- go to next item
finished -- have we seen all items?
stop     -- quit and set finished true
```

The corresponding container object has a function

```
item (it : ITERATOR) : G
```

that returns the item the iterator is currently 'standing on'. If the container also has keys (as do catalogs and dictionaries), then there is also a function

```
key (it : ITERATOR) : K
```

with which one can acquire the key on which the iterator is currently standing.

Armed with this information we are now in a good position to look at an implementation of the routine **overdue**. Here it is:

```
overdue : LIST [BOOK] is

    local
            it1 : ITERATOR
            it2 : ITERATOR
            sl  : SHORT_LIST [BOOK]
            bk  : BOOK

    do
        from
            !!result.make (true)
            it1 := borrowers.iterator
        until
            it1.finished
        loop
            from
                sl  := borrowers.item (it1)
                it2 := sl.iterator
            until
                it2.finished
            loop
                bk := sl.item (it2)

                if bk.date_due < now then
                    result.add (bk)
                end

                it2.forth
            end

            it1.forth
        end
    end
```

The routine consists essentially of two nested loops. In the outer loop the iterator it1 runs over all borrowers in the catalog borrowers. In the inner loop the second iterator it2 runs over the short list of all books that a given borrower has checked out. The date due of a book is compared with now; if it is less, then the book is overdue and is added to the result list result. That's all there is to it.

The only thing about this routine that is a bit mysterious is the entity now. Where did it come from and what does it mean? It is an attribute of the Eiffel/S class SYSTEM_TIME which played a role in our implementation of the class PERSON in Chapter 6. I didn't show you the beginning of the class LIBRARY but now I will:

```
class LIBRARY

inherit
    SYSTEM_TIME

creation
    make
```

As we mentioned in Chapter 6, the value referred to by `now` (a real number) is current Greenwich Mean Time. If the attribute `date_due` in the class `BOOK` also refers to Greenwich Mean Time then the comparison

```
if bk.date_due < now then
```

does what one would expect.

10.5   The user interface

We are now finished with the 'heart' of our program – the part that does the real work. Considering what it does for us, it was surprisingly easy to implement. All that is left to program is the interface to the human user. In many programs, this part is often more work than the rest, and our example is no exception.

In our simple application the root class can provide the interface to the user. It will have a menu that looks something like the following:

```
The commands are :
h : help
a : acquire a book
f : find a book by author
l : lend a book
r : return a book
i : inquire if borrowed
b : which books are borrowed?
o : which books are overdue?
q : end the session
```

For each item in the menu there will be a routine that is called when the user chooses the corresponding menu item. Here is how the routine for 'acquiring a book' could look:

```
acquire is

    local
        author, title, isbn : STRING

    do
```

```
      get_a_string ("author : ")
      author := the_string
      get_a_string ("title  : ")
      title := the_string
      get_a_string ("isbn   : ")
      isbn := the_string

      lib.add_book (isbn, author, title)
   end
```

It uses a procedure `get_a_string` to request the user to enter a string. The value entered is then to be found in `the_string`.

The other routines are similar. The following is the one for borrowing a book:

```
lend is

   local
       bor : STRING
       bk  : BOOK

   do
       get_a_string ("isbn    : ")
       bk := lib.find_with_isbn (the_string)

       if bk = void then
           io.put_string ("Book does not exist%N")

       elseif bk.on_loan then
           io.put_string ("Sorry; book already on loan%N")

       else
           get_a_string ("borrower : ")
           bor := the_string
           get_a_date ("date due : ")
           lib.lend (bk.isbn, bor, the_date)
       end
   end
```

The routine `lend` uses the function `find_with_isbn` from the class LIBRARY to check whether the catalog number entered by the user is really in the library. It then checks to see if the book is in fact already on loan. If not, it then asks for the name of the borrower and the date due and then calls the procedure `lend` in the class LIBRARY.

A program for a real library would almost certainly not ask the user for the date due. Instead, it would add a certain number of days (say 14) to the current date (**now**) and enter that as the date due. However, letting the user specify the date due makes it easier to test our library. We can enter a date due that is already past and then check to see whether the book is reported as overdue.

We show just one more of these routines called in response to the menu choices made by the user. This is the one that reports the books written by a given author and again illustrates the use of iterators:

```
find is

    local
        l    : SHORT_LIST [BOOK]
        it   : ITERATOR

    do
        get_a_string ("author : ")
        l := lib.find_with_author (the_string)

        if l /= void then
            from
                it := l.iterator
            until
                it.finished
            loop
                display_book (l.item (it))
                it.forth
            end

        else
            put_the_string ("We have no books %
                            %from this author%N")
        end
    end
```

We can now safely leave the implementation of the other such routines as an exercise for the reader. We turn to the routines that involve input and output.

We have postulated a class with routines such as `get_a_string` that can be used to ask the user for input. Incidentally, all the routines in the class `LIBRARY` that took a string as argument required that the string be non-void and non-empty. So our routine `get_a_string` had better be programmed to prod the user if he or she tries to enter an empty string. Our hypothetical class is called `INTERACT` and inherits from the Eiffel/S basic class `BASIC_IO` to obtain some low-level input/output routines. This might look as follows:

```
class INTERACT

inherit
    BASIC_IO
```

```
        rename
            put_string  as put_the_string,
            put_int     as put_the_integer,
            put_real    as put_the_real,
            put_bool    as put_the_answer,
            last_string as the_string,
            last_int    as the_integer,
            last_real   as the_real,
            last_bool   as the_answer

        export { NONE}    -- hide the low-level versions
            get_string, get_int, get_real, get_bool
        end

feature

    get_a_string (msg : STRING) is

        local
            done : BOOLEAN

        do
            from
                -- empty statement
            until
                done
            loop
                put_the_string (msg)
                get_string

                if the_string.count > 0 then
                    done := true
                else
                    put_the_string ("Sorry; that wasn't %
                                    %a valid input string%N")
                end
            end
        end

end -- class INTERACT
```

Our routine **get_a_string** uses the procedure **get_string** from the class **BASIC_IO** to do the actual work but it checks that the string is not empty and insists on a non-empty string if the user simply presses <RETURN>.

If our class **INTERACT** is really going to be useful in other applications it will certainly need a few more routines, e.g. for fetching an integer or a real from the user. Here is how the procedure `get_an_integer` might look:

```
get_an_integer (msg : STRING) is

    do
        put_the_string (msg)
        get_string
        the_integer := fmt.s2i (last_string)

    rescue
        put_the_string ("Sorry; that wasn't an integer%N")
        retry
    end
```

It uses an entity `fmt` of type `FORMAT` to convert the string that the user enters into an integer. `FORMAT` is also in the cluster `basic` and provides routines for performing formatted conversion from strings to various kinds of numbers and vice versa. `FORMAT` raises an exception if the string given to `s2i` cannot be interpreted as an integer. Therefore, we catch the exception in a `rescue` clause and ask the user to try again.

Our routine `lend`, above, used a routine `get_a_date` to instruct the user to enter a date as a string and convert it into the internal format used by Eiffel/S. There is no such routine in `BASIC_IO`, so let's put that routine and its partner `date_to_string` into our reusable class `INTERACT` as follows:

```
---------------------------------------------------------

    date_to_string (t : REAL) : STRING is

        do
            to_date (t)
            result := fmt.i2s ("02", month)
            result.append ("/")
            result.append (fmt.i2s ("02", day))
            result.append ("/")
            result.append (fmt.i2s ("04", year))
        end
---------------------------------------------------------


    get_a_date (msg : STRING) is

        local
            tk : TOKENS
            yr : INTEGER
            mn : INTEGER
```

```
                    dy : INTEGER

           do
                    put_the_string (msg)
                    get_string

                    !!tk.make ("/")
                    tk.set_text (last_string)

                    mn := fmt.s2i (tk.token)
                    tk.forth
                    dy := fmt.s2i (tk.token)
                    tk.forth
                    yr := fmt.s2i (tk.token)

                    the_date := to_time (yr, mn, dy, 0, 0, 0)

           rescue
                    put_the_string ("Please enter date as mm/dd/yyyy%N")
                    retry
           end
```

Our class INTERACT will inherit from SYSTEM_TIME and will use the following
features of that class:

```
     to_date (t : REAL)
     to_time (yr, mn, dy, hr, mi, se : INTEGER) : REAL
     year  : INTEGER
     month : INTEGER
     day   : INTEGER
```

The feature to_date sets the attributes year, month, day (as well as hour,
minute, second) according to its argument t. The inverse function to_time
converts its arguments into a time in the internal format.

Our procedure get_a_date uses one other class: TOKENS. This class is prepared
to accept a text string and a string containing a list of 'separators' and then
return the 'tokens' that are contained in the text string and separated by the
'separators'. In our case the only 'separator' is the character '/' (in other national
conventions it might be ':' or '.'). An object of type TOKENS has features token
(the token it is currently on) and forth to cause it to move to the next token, as
well as finished : BOOLEAN to say when it has reached the end of the string.

10.6   Making the library persistent

Our library manager is nearly finished. But there is one last aspect that we have
not yet dealt with. As it stands, our library exists only in main memory. If we

exit from the program all information is forgotten and must be reentered the next time we start the program. How can we make our library 'persistent'? This turns out to be amazingly easy. The answer involves the Eiffel/S class FILE.

The class FILE is a generic class and has a syntax and semantics very close to that of ARRAY. That is, we may regard a file as being essentially a persistent array. In a FILE [G] we can put an object of type G at an arbitrary index n using

    f.put (x, n)

and we can later retrieve it using

    x := f.item (n)

just as with an array. By 'later' we mean not just later in the current session. 'Later' can mean when we start the same program the next day or even in an entirely different program that also uses the type G.

There are of course a few differences between files and arrays. One is that we do not need resize for files. A file automatically grows to the size needed to put an object at a given index. Another is that each call to item returns a *copy* of the item stored at the given index. Thus if we write

    x := f.item (1)
    y := f.item (1)

then x and y will not be equal in the sense of =, although of course

    x.is_equal (y)

will return true.

The call

    f.put (x, n)

stores in the file the object bound to x, together with the whole network of other objects referenced by the attributes of x – its 'friends and relations', so to speak. Then the call

    x := f.item (n)

retrieves this entire network out of the file again – or rather a copy of it.

Now we can solve the problem of making our library persistent in an extremely simple fashion. The routines load_library and store_library handle this problem for us. We will put them into our root class:

```
load_library (lib_name : STRING) is

    local
        f : FILE [LIBRARY]
        h : INTEGER
```

```
    do
        if fs.file_exists (lib_name) then
            h := fs.access_file (lib_name, "rw", false)
            !!f.connect_to (h)
            lib := f.item (1)
            f.disconnect

        else
            fs.add_file (lib_name, "rw")
            !!lib.make
        end
    end
-----------------------------------------------------

store_library (lib_name : STRING) is

    local
        f : FILE [LIBRARY]
        h : INTEGER

    do
        if not fs.file_exists (lib_name) then
            fs.add_file (lib_name, "rw")
        end

        h := fs.access_file (lib_name, "rw", true)
        !!f.connect_to (h)
        f.put (lib, 1)
        f.disconnect
    end
```

The most important lines here are

```
    lib := f.item (1)
```

and

```
    f.put (lib, 1)
```

That is, we poke the entire library into our file at index 1 and later retrieve it
again – also at index 1 of course.

But what's all the rest? In order for an object of type FILE to persist it has
to be connected to a file in a sense that the operating system understands. The
Eiffel/S class that manages this connection is FILE_SYSTEM and the entity fs
that appears above is of type FILE_SYSTEM.

In the routine `load_library`, this object `fs` is asked to find out if the file with name `lib_name` exists. If so, an object `f` of type `FILE [LIBRARY]` is created and connected to the physical file. Then the object of type `LIBRARY` at index 1 is fetched from the file and the file disconnected again. If the physical file does not yet exist it is created along with an empty object of type `LIBRARY`.

The routine `store_library` is even simpler. It creates an object `f` of type

```
FILE [LIBRARY]
```

and connects it to the physical file `lib_name` (which it creates if the file does not yet exist). Then it puts our library into the file at index 1. Finally `f` is disconnected from the physical file.

Our library manager is now complete. All in all it really was not very difficult to build.

10.7   Exercises

1. Add a routine to the library program with which a user can inquire which books a given borrower currently has checked out.
2. Producing an index for a book is often a very tedious process. Suppose you already have a utility that extracts all index references from your book and produces a file having one line for each such reference. The lines are in the format

   ```
   {keyword}{p}
   ```

   where 'keyword' stands for a key word or phrase that is to appear in the index and p is the number of the page on which the reference occurs.
   Write an Eiffel program that reads this file and produces a second file with lines of the form

   ```
   keyword, p1, p2, ..., pk
   ```

   where $p1, p2, \ldots, pk$ are the numbers of all the pages on which the key word or phrase 'keyword' appears. The lines in this second file should be ordered lexicographically and the page numbers $p1, p2, \ldots, pk$ are to be in increasing order.
   (Hint: you are likely to find the Eiffel/S classes `TEXTFILE`, `SORTED_LIST` and `SORTED_CATALOG` very useful for this exercise.)

Chapter 11

Simulating Digital Circuits

11.1 The model

One of the primary uses of software is to simulate some aspect of our physical
or mental world: a population of bacteria, an organic molecule or a system of
non-linear equations. There are many reasons why simulation in software is
advantageous such as the following:

- The process of abstraction and simplification needed to make a model in
  software often results in a better understanding of the domain being inves-
  tigated.
- It is usually much less expensive to investigate a software model of an
  object than to investigate the object itself.

The grandfather of all object-oriented languages is Simula, and, as the name
suggests, Simula was originally developed for use in simulation. Even today, simulation is an area in which object-oriented languages seem particularly suitable.

To illustrate the use of object-oriented methods in building a simulation we
shall construct a simulation of digital circuits. Our model will only simulate a
few aspects of such circuits, but it could easily be extended to model additional
aspects as well.

What are the objects that we need to model? The following are two that occur
to us immediately:

1. Logical elements providing a well defined logical function. Such an element
   could, for example, form the logical *and* of its two inputs and put the result
   on to its output. Such elements will be referred to by the generic name
   gate. Each gate can have several inputs and several outputs.

   To model an important aspect of real circuits we do not assume that a gate
   computes its function and sets its outputs instantaneously. Instead, each
   gate has a characteristic **delay** – a period that must pass between the time
   a new signal is detected at an input and the time the outputs all have their
   new values.

139

2. Wires for connecting the gates. A wire carries a **signal**. Since we are concerned with digital circuits here, we restrict the signals to the values 0 and 1. A wire has two ends of course, but we shall also think of a wire as having a direction: its input end is attached to the output of just one gate and its output end is attached to the inputs of arbitrarily many gates.

In our model we shall think of a wire as knowing its 'clients'; these are the gates to whose inputs the output end of the wire is connected. In the same way, each gate will know which wire is connected to each of its outputs. Signals will now propagate through the circuit as follows:

1. When a gate has a new output value ready (after the appropriate delay) it informs the wires attached to its outputs.
2. When a wire is informed of a new signal at its input end, it checks to see if the new value is different from the old one. If so, it sets the new value and informs all its clients of the change.
3. When a client gate is informed that the signal at one of its inputs has changed, it 'sets the alarm clock' for its characteristic delay and does nothing further for the moment.
4. When the 'alarm goes off', the gate calculates the new values for its outputs and repeats step 1.

There will of course be many different kinds of gates with differing logical functions such as *and*, *or*, *not*, etc., but the description given above shows that they all have a certain commonality in their behavior. This is the typical situation requiring an abstract class that will have many descendents.

11.2   The class WIRE

We begin with the simplest of our building blocks, the wires. The description given above makes it clear what properties and behavior a wire will need: it will have a signal (BOOLEAN) and a list of 'clients', i.e. objects of type GATE. It will need procedures with which it can be informed of a new client and with which the gate attached to its input end can inform it of a new value. We can now write down the class without further ado:

```
class WIRE

creation
    make

feature

    signal : BOOLEAN
```

```
    make is

        do
            !!connections.make (false)
                -- argument 'false' means duplicates allowed
        end
------------------------------------------------------

    set_signal (new_signal : BOOLEAN) is
                -- set 'signal' to 'new_signal' and
                -- inform all connected gates

        local
            it : ITERATOR

        do
            if new_signal /= signal then
                signal := new_signal

                from
                    it := connections.iterator
                until
                    it.finished
                loop
                    connections.item (it).trigger
                    it.forth
                end
            end
        end
------------------------------------------------------

    connect_to (g : GATE) is
            -- connect 'current' to gate 'g'

        do
            connections.add (g)
        end
------------------------------------------------------

feature { NONE }

    connections : SHORT_LIST [GATE]

end -- class WIRE
```

We have assumed here that every object of type `GATE` has a procedure `trigger` with which it can be informed that one of its inputs has changed. Otherwise, the class `WIRE` is perfectly straightforward.

11.3   The class GATE

Now we deal with the abstract class `GATE` which expresses properties and behavior that are common to all gates. As we have just seen it must provide a procedure `trigger` that can be called by the wires connected to its inputs. The description of signal propagation given above makes it clear that the routine `trigger` merely has the job of setting the alarm clock.

In addition, every gate will need a procedure – say `activate` – that can be called by the alarm clock when the specified delay has elapsed. This procedure must carry out the actual work of the gate: recalculate the values of the outputs and inform the wires connected to them. Since the job of this routine `activate` varies according to the type of gate, it will be a deferred routine to be made effective in each effective gate.

We could now write an abstract class with the two routines `trigger` and `activate`. That is probably how one would proceed if one had never programmed a simulation before. Experience with simulations, however, shows that the mechanism of an 'alarm clock' that activates an object after some specified delay is needed in many situations. Therefore, it would be short-sighted to build an alarm clock that could only activate gates. For this reason we add a further level of abstraction: a class `ACTOR` that has a procedure `activate` that can be called by alarm clocks. That is all the class `ACTOR` has. Here it is:

```
deferred class ACTOR

feature

    activate is
            -- Called by the scheduler
            -- when the delay has elapsed.
            -- This procedure defines what
            -- the actor actually does.

        deferred
        end

end -- class ACTOR
```

We are not yet ready to think about how a clock or scheduler could be implemented. But we do know that we want all elements in our simulation to use the *same* clock and this is a typical situation for a **once** function. So we introduce a corresponding class `THE_CLOCK`:

```
class THE_CLOCK

feature

    clock : SCHEDULER is
            -- sharable clock

        once
            !!result.make
        end

end -- class THE_CLOCK
```

We further postulate that a scheduler will at least have a procedure

```
    schedule (client : ACTOR, delay : INTEGER)
```

with which a client can request to be 'awakened' after a given delay.

With this information we can now program our abstract class **GATE**:

```
deferred class GATE

inherit
    ACTOR;
    THE_CLOCK

feature

    trigger is
            -- Called by an attached wire
            -- when its signal changes.

        do
            clock.schedule (current, delay)
        end
----------------------------------------------------

feature { NONE }

    delay : INTEGER

end -- class GATE
```

To illustrate the kind of class that will be derived from **GATE**, we now describe one of the basic building blocks of any digital circuit: the nand-gate. Its logical function is to form the logical *and* of its two inputs and put the negation of the result on to its output (nand = not and).

The class **NANDGATE** will of course be derived from **GATE** and will make the routine **activate** effective. It will have three attributes of type **WIRE**: one for each of the two inputs and one for the output. It will also need a creation procedure **make** with which it can be informed of its connections. The class **NANDGATE** is as follows:

```
class NANDGATE

inherit
    GATE
        redefine
            activate
        end

creation
    make

feature

    make (i1, i2, o : WIRE) is
            -- create nand gate with inputs i1, i2, output o

        do
            delay := 2
            in1   := i1
            in2   := i2
            out   := o

            in1.connect_to (current)
            in2.connect_to (current)

            activate
        end
-------------------------------------------------------

    activate is
            -- set out to in1 nand in2

        do
            out.set_signal (not (in1.signal and in2.signal))
        end
-------------------------------------------------------

feature { NONE }
```

```
    in1 : WIRE
    in2 : WIRE
    out : WIRE
```

end -- class NANDGATE

We have stipulated arbitrarily that the delay for a nand-gate should be two time units. One can experiment later to see the effect of giving the various kinds of gates differing delays.

The creation procedure **make** informs the wires connected to the two inputs that **current** is now one of their clients. Then **activate** is called to set the proper value at the output.

The reader will now surely feel quite up to programming an and-gate and an or-gate as well as an inverter (logical not).

11.4 The scheduler

Now we need to think about how the scheduler should look. Once we have solved that problem we can start running simulations.

The first remark that needs to be made is that we are not trying to carry out realtime simulations here. Thus the 'time' used by our scheduler need not have any relation to the system time, for example. The scheduler can have an attribute **time : INTEGER** that represents the concept of time for the given simulation. If the scheduler discovers that the next activity to be carried out is to occur at time t_1, then it simply sets its attribute **time** to the value t_1 and starts the activity in question – thereby 'saving time' by 'skipping over' the required interval.

We already know that our scheduler must have a procedure **schedule** with which a client can request to be activated after a certain delay. The only other routine that is needed in our simple simulation is a procedure – say **run** – with which the controller of the simulation can start the clock (and the simulation) running. The scheduler or clock will then activate the first client on its list, which in turn will probably cause other clients to make requests to the clock. This process will continue until either the clock has no more jobs to do or else for ever.

The only question still to be decided is how the scheduler should organize its jobs in such a way that it can easily find the one to be carried out next. This is a typical situation for using a *priority queue*. A priority queue is not organized by the FIFO (first in/first out) principle. Instead, each entry in the queue has a priority (integer or real) and the queue is always ordered in such a way that the element with maximal priority is at the front of the queue.

Does the Eiffel/S library provide priority queues? Again we look into the cluster **contain** and find two: one in which the elements have a total order and thus provide their 'priority' themselves, and one in which the priority is provided separately as a 'key'. This second class seems to be what we want, so we shall use it in our scheduler.

There is only one point at which we need to take care: a priority queue always keeps the element with *highest* priority at the front. But the next activity is the one with the *lowest* time. This is no real problem though; we simply use the negative time as priority!

Here now is our class SCHEDULER:

```
class SCHEDULER

creation
    make

feature

    time : INTEGER

-----------------------------------------------------

    make is

        do
            !!jobs.make
        end
-----------------------------------------------------

    schedule (client : ACTOR; delay : INTEGER) is
            -- schedule client to be activated after delay

        do
            jobs.add (-(time + delay), client)
        end
-----------------------------------------------------

    run is
            -- initiate all scheduled events

        do
            from
                -- empty clause
            until
                jobs.empty
            loop
                time := -jobs.key
                jobs.item.activate
```

```
                    jobs.remove
              end
        end
--------------------------------------------------------
```

feature { NONE }

   jobs : KEY_PRIORITY_QUEUE [INTEGER, ACTOR]

end -- class SCHEDULER

There is one small problem with our scheduler: it runs until the system sta-
bilizes, i.e. until there are no more jobs for it to do. But if we build a circuit
that oscillates, then it will never stabilize in this sense and so the routine run
will never stop. We won't worry about that problem here, but one could alter
run to accept an argument max_time :   INTEGER and to run only until time >
max_time holds.

11.5   An adder

The secret of building complex systems – whether in hardware or software – is to
build ever higher levels of abstraction where each level uses objects of the next
lower level of abstraction as its building blocks. We shall do just that with our
gates. To illustrate this process we first build a one bit adder. Then we shall use
it to build an n bit adder.

A one bit adder has inputs a and b for the addends and c_{in} for the carry bit
from the previous addition. The outputs are *sum* and c_{out} for the sum bit and
the carry bit. The one bit adder can be constructed from three nand gates and
two xor gates (exclusive or) according to the Figure 11.1. The reader who is not
familiar with digital circuits can convince himself that this circuit does what it
is supposed to do by setting up the truth table for the circuit or by trying out
sample inputs.

Here, then, is the class BIT_ADDER.

```
class BIT_ADDER

inherit
    GATE
        redefine
            activate
        end
```

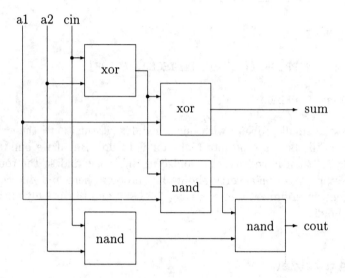

Figure 11.1 A 1-bit adder

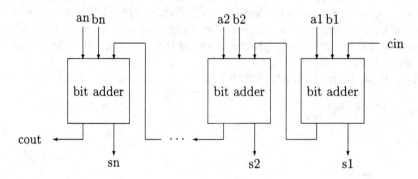

Figure 11.2 A full adder

```
creation
    make

feature

    make (a1, a2, cin, sum, cout : WIRE) is
            -- create 1-bit adder

        local
            x, y, z    : WIRE
            o1, o2     : XORGATE
            n1, n2, n3 : NANDGATE

        do
            !!x.make
            !!y.make
            !!z.make

            !!o1.make (a2, cin, x)
            !!o2.make (x, a1, sum)
            !!n1.make (x, a1, y)
            !!n2.make (a2, cin, z)
            !!n3.make (y, z, cout)
        end
--------------------------------------------------------

    activate is

        do
            -- never called!
        end

end -- class BIT_ADDER
```

Now that we can add one bit we can 'chain' n such one bit adders to obtain an adder that is capable of adding two n-bit numbers. The circuit diagram is shown in Figure 11.2. This is not the most efficient way to add two n-bit numbers because the carry bits have to 'ripple' through from the least significant bit to the most significant bit. But it will work and illustrates nicely the principal of building complex elements out of simpler ones.

The class FULL_ADDER, which can add two four-bit numbers, now looks as follows:

```
class FULL_ADDER

inherit
    GATE
        redefine
            activate
        end

creation
    make

feature

    make (a1, a2, a3, a4,
          b1, b2, b3, b4,
          s1, s2, s3, s4,
          cin, cout : WIRE) is

        local
            c1, c2, c3    : WIRE
            d1, d2, d3, d4 : BIT_ADDER

        do
            !!c1.make
            !!c2.make
            !!c3.make

            !!d1.make (a1, b1, cin, s1, c1)
            !!d2.make (a2, b2, c1, s2, c2)
            !!d3.make (a3, b3, c2, s3, c3)
            !!d4.make (a4, b4, c3, s4, cout)
        end
-------------------------------------------------------

    activate is

        do
            -- never called!
        end

end -- class FULL_ADDER
```

We could now write a program to test our new adder interactively. The most tedious part is creating the fourteen wires needed as inputs and outputs for the adder. We can make our lives a little simpler by bundling wires to 'cables', as in the following class:

```
class CABLE4     -- a cable with four wires

creation
    make

feature

    make is

        local
            i : INTEGER
            x : WIRE

        do
            from
                !!w.make (0, 3)
            until
                i > 3
            loop
                !!x.make
                w.put (x, i)
                i := i + 1
            end
        end
-------------------------------------------------------

    w1 : WIRE is

        do
            result := w.item (0)
        end
-------------------------------------------------------

    w2, w3, w4 similarly ...

-------------------------------------------------------

    signal : INTEGER is

        local
            i : INTEGER

        do
```

```
            from
                i := 3
            until
                i < 0
            loop
                if w.item (i).signal then
                    result := 2 * result + 1
                else
                    result := 2 * result
                end

                i := i - 1
            end
        end
-----------------------------------------------------------


    set_signal (n : INTEGER) is

        require
            four_bit : 0 <= n and then n < 16
        local
            i, m : INTEGER

        do
            from
                m := n
            until
                i > 3
            loop
                if (m \\ 2) = 0 then
                    w.item (i).set_signal (false)
                else
                    w.item (i).set_signal (true)
                end

                m := m // 2
                i := i + 1
            end
        end
-----------------------------------------------------------
feature { NONE }

    w : ARRAY [WIRE]

end -- class CABLE4
```

Now that we have such a class it would be sensible to provide FULL_ADDER with a second creation procedure

```
make_with_cables (a, b, s : CABLE4, cin, cout : WIRE)
```

Now our interactive test program is reasonably simple. We make it the root class, as follows:

```
class TESTADD

inherit
    INTERACT;
    THE_CLOCK

creation
    make

feature

    a, b, s : CABLE4   -- 's' is the sum
    low_cin : WIRE     -- held 'low'
    carry   : WIRE


------------------------------------------------------------


    build_circuit is

        local
            adder : FULL_ADDER

        do
            !!a.make
            !!b.make
            !!s.make
            !!low_cin.make
            low_cin.set_signal (false)
            !!carry.make
            !!adder.make_with_cables (a, b, s, low_cin, carry)
        end
------------------------------------------------------------

    make is

        local
            sum : INTEGER
```

```
        do
            build_circuit

            get_an_integer ("First summand  : ")
            a.set_signal (the_integer)
            get_an_integer ("Second summand : ")
            b.set_signal (the_integer)

            clock.run

            if carry.signal then
                sum := s.signal + 16
            else
                sum := s.signal
            end

            put_the_string ("The sum        : ")
            put_the_integer (sum)
            put_a_newline
            put_the_string ("The time       : ")
            put_the_integer (clock.time)
            put_a_newline
        end

end -- class TESTADD
```

Note The class INTERACT from which our class TESTADD inherits is the class we created in Chapter 10 to provide interactive input at a slightly higher level than that provided by BASIC_IO.

With this program we can add any two integers in the range 0 to 15 and obtain a result in the range 0 to 30.

11.6   Exercises

1. Our routine `activate` in the descendents of GATE uses the most recent values of the inputs in order to compute the values of the outputs. This is unrealistic; the point to a delay is that changes at the inputs need a certain amount of time to propagate through the internal circuits of a gate before they reach the outputs. Therefore `activate` really ought to use the input values that prevailed at the time when `trigger` was called. Modify your model to make it behave in this more realistic manner.

2. Program a class LED. It should have an attribute `name` that is set by the creation procedure `make`. It should have one input and no outputs and

whenever the signal at its input changes it should respond (without delay) by printing its name on the display, together with the new value of its signal.

3. Program an RS-flipflop. It you don't know what an RS-flipflop is, you'll find it in any book on digital circuits. It can easily be constructed from two nand-gates.

   Now write a root class to test your RS-flipflop interactively by asking the user for the values for the two inputs r and s. The two outputs should be connected to objects of type LED with names q and q_.

4. The ambitious reader who has some experience with digital circuits may now want to try her hand at programming a multiplier that can multiply two four-bit numbers obtaining an eight-bit product.

The last four exercises deal with constraint propagation. An equation such as

$$9c = 5(f - 32)$$

in which variables c, f occur can be regarded as a **constraint** on the set of value pairs (c, f): one only considers pairs that satisfy the equation. In the case above, it is possible, given any value for c, to solve the equation for a corresponding value of f. With non-linear equations this will often not be possible, but the point of view that the equation (or, more generally, system of equations) constrains the set of possible values of the variables is quite generally valid.

We can consider a constraint as an object with 'inputs'. Each 'input' can have a value (type REAL) or it can be indeterminate. When the constraint is activated it attempts to compute the values of those inputs which are still indeterminate from the values of those that already have values.

There is in fact a clear analogy with the gates in our network simulation. However, we have no delays here and no distinction between 'input' and 'output'. Any input can become an output if its value was originally indeterminate; its new value is calculated on the basis of the values of the other inputs.

We can, of course, construct complicated constraints out of simpler ones if we also introduce **connectors**. The connectors play a role similar to that of the wires in the network simulation. A connector has a (possibly indeterminate) value and can be connected to arbitrarily many constraints. If the value of a connector is altered from outside (user) or by one of the constraints, then it activates each of the other constraints with which it is connected. Hence, the equation above could be illustrated by the the diagram in Fig. 11.3 (cf. [Ref. 4], p. 232).

5. Program a class CONNECTOR with public features

```
value      : REAL
has_value  : BOOLEAN
```

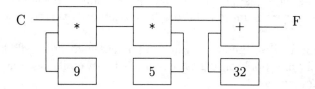

Figure 11.3 A constraint propagator

```
connect_to (c : CONSTRAINT)
set_value (v : REAL; setter : CONSTRAINT)
forget_value (retractor : CONSTRAINT)
```

set_value is to raise an exception if an attempt is made to alter a value that is not indeterminate. forget_value only 'forgets' a value if retractor is the constraint that originally set the value. Otherwise, forget_value does nothing; in particular it does not raise an exception.

6. Program an abstract class CONSTRAINT with public features

```
propagate_value
forget_values
```

propagate_value is the routine that tries to set the values of the still indeterminate inputs on the basis of the already set values.

From this class you should then derive 'primitive' constraint classes

ADDER, MULTIPLIER, CONSTANT, PROBE

A PROBE can be used to display the value of a connector. Its creation procedure

```
make (c : CONNECTOR; text : STRING)
```

is passed a text as argument that is then displayed by propagate_value and forget_values, together with the current value of c respectively 'no value'.

7. Write a root class TEMPERATURE that permits the user to test the constraint given above interactively and thus to convert Centigrade temperatures into Fahrenheit, and vice versa. The user must, of course, be given the possibility of 'forgetting' values that have previously been set.

8. Write a root class PYTHAGORAS that permits the user to test the equation

$$x^2 + y^2 = z^2$$

interactively.

References

[Ref. 1] Bertrand Meyer, *Object-oriented Software Construction*, Prentice Hall, 1988.

[Ref. 2] Bertrand Meyer, *Eiffel: The Language*, Prentice Hall, 1991.

[Ref. 3] Jon Bentley, *Programming Pearls*, Addison Wesley, 1986.

[Ref. 4] Harold Abelson and Gerald Jay Sussman, *Structure and Interpretation of Computer Programs*, MIT Press, 1985.

Index